WAR AND HOPE

THE CASE FOR CAMBODIA

WAR AND HOPE

THE CASE FOR CAMBODIA

PRINCE NORODOM SIHANOUK

TRANSLATED BY MARY FEENEY

 PANTHEON BOOKS, NEW YORK

Library of Congress Cataloging in Publication Data
Norodom Sihanouk Varman, King of Cambodia, 1922–
War and hope.
Translation of Chroniques de guerre . . . et d'espoir.
1. Cambodia—Foreign relations. 2. Cambodia—
Neutrality. I. Title.
DS554.8.N6613 1980   959.6'04   79-3609
ISBN 0-394-51115-8

Grateful acknowledgment is given to The Associated Press,
New York, for permission to use excerpts from a March 6,
1979, report quoting a statement by Richard Holbrooke and
an April 2, 1979, cable of Senator Edward Kennedy.

Manufactured in the United States of America
Designed by Joy Chu

First American Edition

THIS BOOK IS DEDICATED
TO MY BELOVED KHMER PEOPLE,
WHOSE SUFFERING IS UNPARALLELED
IN HUMAN HISTORY: A PEOPLE
NOW IN ITS DEATH THROES DUE TO.
THE UNCHECKED CONFLICT BETWEEN
TWO TYPES OF COMMUNISM.

Norodom Sihanouk of Cambodia

You must continue the good works I have done, for
they are also yours.
—Edict of the Hospitals of Jayavarman VII,
Sey Fong stele

The odds for peace must be swiftly helped to outweigh
the odds for war.
—Norodom Sihanouk, in a speech at the
First Conference of Indochinese Peoples,
February 14, 1965

Temples sleep in the forest
Recalling the greatness of Moha Nokor
Like rock, the Khmer race is eternal
Let us trust in the fate of Kampuchea
The Empire defying time . . .
—From the Nokoreach

CONTENTS

CONTENTS

FOREWORD

An ancestral prophecy predicts that one day the unfortunate Khmer people will be forced to choose between being eaten by tigers or swallowed by crocodiles. Today we are seeing that prophecy fulfilled in the most tragic way possible. The Kampuchean people are on the brink of extinction, dying a slow death, murdered in the name of two conflicting types of Communism. It is a struggle to the death between Kampuchean and Vietnamese Communism; it is also a dispute between the two Communist giants they represent, China and Russia.

As the author of this book, I certainly do not pretend to have written a work of history. But since the force of circumstances has placed me in an exceptional situation in regard to events involving the Khmer Rouge, Chinese, and North Vietnamese one after the other, or one against the other, I believe history should have my personal testimony on a tragedy that continues even now to bathe my unfortunate country in blood.

My readers will not find a complete exposé on the conflict in question here. Nor will they be given a detailed description of the Hanoi "blitzkrieg" against Pol Pot's army (late December, 1978, and early January, 1979). The international press has already dealt with this; I will confine myself to complementing what has been said in newspapers and books with my own information and commentary.

In conclusion, I will sketch what I consider a possible solution to the thorny problem of Khmer-Vietnam relations.

Today, considering how intolerable the situation is, how surely it will bring about the extermination of the Khmer race in the middle or long term, I hope my services can aid in the attempt to find a solution. Although I propose what I consider a logical and reasonable answer to the problem of Khmer-Vietnam relations, it can be nothing but a dream unless the foreign powers implicated in the devastating war in Kampuchea, directly or otherwise, grant the supremely unlucky Khmer people the right to self-determination.

During the 1960s Marcel Talabot made a remarkable film on Cambodia for the *Connaissance du Monde* travel documentary series. It was called "The Smiling Country." Today we can view it as an historical document. Phnom Penh, once fabulous, flourishing, a pleasant city to live in, has now become a ghost town. A complex, hierarchic society, strongly rooted in the moral teachings of Buddhism such as nonviolence and respect for others, has been brutally torn apart, shattered into ten thousand different kinds of barbarism. What organization there is sees the people as slaves to work on mad schemes such as reconstructing the pryamids, conquering neighboring countries, teaching the entire world a lesson in civilization.

"How on earth have things come to this?" the foreigner asks himself, uncomprehending. Aghast at the evidence provided by the tens of thousands of refugees who were less than content with the new Cambodian government, the commentator seeks a logical analysis, tries out different hypotheses.

A first-rate witness was in Cambodia for the past four years: Prince Norodom Sihanouk. From January, 1976, until January, 1979, the country's former head of state was living—or rather, surviving—under house arrest. He was first confined to the Khemarin Palace, the former guest residence for visiting foreign dignitaries, then to a modern house right next to the royal palace in the center of Phnom Penh. He spent part of his time, along with his wife, Neak Monéang Monique Sihanouk, and his two sons, the Princes Sihamoni and Norindrapong—a faked telegram had summoned them back to Phnom Penh in April, 1976[1]—and a very limited retinue, looking through the contents of the Palace library, which had not been damaged. A radio kept him in touch with the world. He listened to the dithyrambics of Phnom Penh's new masters, the Khmer Rouge, about whom we foreigners know so little. He was also able to tune in broadcasts from the BBC, the Voice of America, and France Inter. This is how Sihanouk learned that the whole world was wondering what had become of him (a fact that only added to his suffering): some reports said he had been executed, others that he was seriously ill or afflicted with deafness, stammering. Day by day, Sihanouk kept notes.

The rare visitors to the Cambodian capital at that time were told by the Khmer Rouge leadership that the Prince was busy writing his memoirs and did not want to see anyone.

It would be interesting to know whether or not the Prince's mind was enough at ease for him to ponder a rather exceptional destiny: his own. He has said that often when he went to bed at night he did not know if he would wake up in the morning. His guards were young Khmer Rouge, recently trained to torture; with no human victims handy, they practiced on domestic animals. In isolation, the Prince received no news of his countrymen, his friends, the scattered members of his own family. Penn Nouth, his faithful adviser, former Prime Minister of the GRUNK (Cambodian Royal Government of National Union) met with Sihanouk only once, during an official banquet Pol Pot gave in 1978, ostensibly for the purpose of having his staff

[1] One of the princes was studying in Pyong Yang, the other in Moscow. The Khmer Rouge sent a telegram signed "Sihanouk" asking them to come home.

photographer take pictures of the Prince to satisfy the international press. Other former GRUNK ministers were also present at the banquet: Sarin Chhak, former ambassador to Egypt, then Foreign Affairs Minister, and Defense Minister General Duong Sam Ol, both looking "pale and thin." No one knows what happened to them since.

Cambodia had become a fragmented country. Every facet of interpersonal relationships was subjected to the ideological prism of the party in power. Every person was a potential traitor. Twelve-year-old children were drafted into the army, separated from their families, pushed into acting as cadres with the power of life and death over their charges. The communications network, the mail, the telephone had stopped working; it was every man for himself. Pity, compassion, charity, love, happiness, were meaningless words. The individual was no more than an antlike worker in a regimented society. Norodom Sihanouk, removed from power, was a citizen like any other: a pawn in the Khmer Rouge's overextended game.

The only contact the prince had with the government was through Khieu Samphan, the "President of the Presidium," one of Sihanouk's former ministers. And then of course only the government had the right to initiate dialogue; from time to time Khieu Samphan would invite "Citizen" Sihanouk and his wife on a tour of the country's cooperatives. He no doubt made every effort to show the Prince the regime's finest. Yet it was painful for Norodom Sihnouk to see his countrymen recognize him, wave to him, try to pass messages to him. There was nothing he could do, except hope for a better future . . . for his people.

The Khmer Rouge regime was out of touch with reality. Its leaders had teeming brains but hearts of stone. No doubt as young students in Paris they did not fully digest the theoretical rudiments of Marxism they picked up in the

Latin Quarter. Norodom Sihanouk even suspects that Pol Pot confused *Das Kapital* with *Mein Kampf.* Hitler's name often came up in the speeches of this paunchy little man with the sly smile, who always wanted to go one better, take things farther, with the slogan "This is the final fight, let us make a clean sweep of the past . . ."

The past, the fabulous heritage of Khmer civilization, one of the world's oldest and most prestigious, was something Pol Pot clearly intended to destroy. He went so far as to have objects used in Buddhist temple services melted down, then use the metal for statues of himself. His ambition was to build a specific "Pol Pot" civilization by means of a refined brand of collectivism.

Was Pol Pot a dictator? Were the Khmer Rouge really Hitlerites? At the beginning, it was more than anything a family affair: Pol Pot's number-two man, Ieng Sary, was related to him by marriage: Mme. Ieng Sary, née Khieu Thirith, was Mme. Pol Pot's younger sister. Both women also held cabinet posts. The two couples wielded all, or nearly all, actual power in the country; they *were* the *Angka*, the Organization. What about other figures? They had minor roles, without much breadth or authority: Khieu Samphan, an intellectual, was President of the Presidium, largely an honorary title. Son Sen was in charge of the armed forces. Hou Yuon and Hu Nim, probably too independent, were executed. Three brothers of aristocratic background, Thiounn Thieunn, a doctor, Thiounn Mumm, a graduate of France's prestigious *École Polytechnique,* and Thiounn Prasith, an engineer, had become so-called "poor peasants" and were too dependent to merit execution; they were devoted body and soul to the two dictators.

The history of the anti-Sihanouk rebellion really began as early as 1941 with Son Ngoc Thanh, one of the founders of the Khmer Issarak ("Free Khmer") movement. Warped by ambition, he was an early and obstinate opponent of the monarchy.

Son Ngoc Thanh, born December 7, 1908 at Ky La in the province of Tra Ving, South Vietnam, wasted no time aligning himself with the Japanese Occupation forces after his attempted coup d'état failed in 1942. The Japanese named him Minister of Foreign Affairs on June 1, 1945; a month and a half later he eliminated the rest of the cabinet and named himself the first head of an allegedly independent Cambodia. To top things off, he organized a plebiscite in which he won 100 percent of the vote . . . with blank ballots.

France's General Leclerc arrested him on October 16, 1945, for anti-Allied activities. He returned to Cambodia on October 29, 1951, and founded the newspaper *Khmer Krok*. Publication was suspended in February, 1952. He once again joined the *maquis* on March 9, 1952, and attempted to revive the Khmer Issarak insurrection, later returning as a dissident.

The most serious observers of the Cambodian scene estimate that at the time he could not have had more than a few hundred followers. When he returned to Phnom Penh in 1954, at King Norodom Sihanouk's personal request to French authorities, Son Ngoc Thanh hatched new plots against the monarchy. From 1956 on, he worked with Sam Sary, former deputy Prime Minister and Ambassador to England, to create the Khmer Serei (also "Free Khmer") movement, supported by the CIA, South Vietnam, Laos, and Thailand. In 1958, Son Ngoc Thanh was implicated in the plot by the governor of Siem Reap province, Chhuon Mchulpich, known as "Dap Chhuon," to have his province and Battambang secede from Cambodia and join Thailand. He was also mentioned in connection with the bombing attempt on the Chief of Protocol in the throne room of the royal palace, on August 31, 1959.

In the national referendum of June 5, 1960, the head of the Khmer Serei movement won 133 votes to Norodom Sihanouk's 2,020,349.

We have seen that the Khmer Rouge was a family affair. One might say as much about the Khmer Issarak Liberation Front, headed from 1950 on by Son Ngoc Minh, a relative of Son Ngoc Thanh's (one of the Khmer Serei leader's brothers, Son Thai Nguyen, was also elected to the South Vietnam Senate). The putative father of a dissident movement, Son Ngoc Minh became the head of the Khmer Vietminh. Following the Geneva agreements of 1954, they went over to Hanoi.

Only under extraordinary circumstances could any of Cambodia's variety of tiny minority groups have come to power. Son Ngoc Thanh was a beneficiary of Lon Nol's March, 1970 coup. He became Prime Minister for a few months, serving as the government's link with the CIA, just as he had worked with the Japanese during World War II. This time the cost was 800,000 dead in an atrocious war and a deadly pounding by the U.S. Air Force.

The elderly Son Ngoc Minh, eliminated by the Khmer Rouge in 1972, did not fully taste the fruits of his plotting. His successors, even if they deny it, are Heng Samrin and his pro-Vietnamese cohorts, who moved into Phnom Penh when Hanoi invaded the city in January, 1979.

As for the four Latin Quarter conspirators—Saloth Sar (alias Pol Pot, his pseudonym), Ieng Sary, and their wives, all of whom came from the bourgeoisie and were certainly not "poor peasants"—they came to the fore in the mess left by Lon Nol and Son Ngoc Thanh, and paved the way for Heng Samrin. The final and awful result: 1,500,000 Khmers killed in three years (1975–1978), a devastated country.

That is the story of anti-Sihanouk movements over the last thirty years, brought to power only through foreign intervention.

Cambodia's history is unfortunately replete with plots and counterplots, conquests and occupations, secret conspiracies. Wedged between the Annamites and the Siamese, the ancient Khmer Empire commanded their respect. It stretched from the Point of Camau, the extreme southern tip of Indochina, to near the site of Bangkok. Little by little the Empire disintegrated. On August 11, 1863, the French Admiral Lagrandière forced King Norodom to sign a protectorate treaty. On July 17, 1884, the kingdom further capitulated in order to survive: the Governor of Cochin China, Charles Thomson, arrived in Phnom Penh, threatened the Khmer sovereign with deportation, and forced him to sign a protectorate treaty under which he relinquished judicial, financial, military, and diplomatic powers.

One of the young King Norodom Sihanouk's primary concerns when he succeeded his grandfather, King Sisowath Monivong, on April 23, 1941, was to make his country completely independent. A first agreement between Phnom Penh and Paris, on January 7, 1946, recognized Cambodia's internal autonomy, then its *de jure* independence on November 8, 1949. King Norodom Sihanouk's nonviolent crusade led to the winning of national independence on November 9, 1953. A few months later, another campaign, dubbed "Samakki," mobilized the population against occupation of Cambodian territory by Vietminh troops. It succeeded, as Prince Sihanouk later put it, "without a shot being fired."

In this way at the first Geneva Conference on Indochina, in July, 1954, the kingdom of Cambodia was able to appear as a united, free, and sovereign country, and thus avoid partition of the kind that slowly brought the two neighboring countries, Vietnam and Laos, to ruin.

What obscure impulse, then, led the young king Norodom Sihanouk to abdicate on March 3, 1955, less than a month after he had scored an overwhelming victory in a national referendum? Officially, he wanted to free himself of the yoke of royal privileges and rituals, which he found suffocating, to grow closer to his people and create the ideal conditions for building a true democratic regime. To this end he founded the Sangkum Reastr Niyum, the People's Socialist Community party, its broad base intended to replace a system of parties too closely modeled on Western political regimes. But the truth is the King had been "crowned," so to speak, by the French Admiral Decoux, and his first concern was not to owe his throne to any foreign power, including France, and to seek his legitimacy through the people.

This concern for independence was to haunt him continually, for his country and for his people. It would be the very base of his policy of nonalignment and neutrality, a principle he would never stray from while at the same time refusing to turn it into an ideological dogma.

A number of leitmotivs are evident in the Prince's career. They have guided his conduct through the fluctuations of current events and allowed him to keep Cambodia at peace both at home and abroad for nearly two decades, a rare achievement in his country's difficult history.

The first is his deep belief in the virtues of Buddhism. "It is because he preaches all the virtues a citizen or a nation could hope to display . . . particularly honesty, temperance, frankness, pacifism, unselfishness, altruism, and equality among all men and all castes (differences between them should be based solely on their own specific merits and their good or bad deeds), that we have raised Buddhism to the rank of our State religion, and that we have patterned our socialism after it," Sihanouk wrote in the review *Kambuja* in December, 1965. He continued: "Such a doctrine, applied to our domestic and foreign policy, means the Khmers are warriors fighting for the people's happiness, for peace, freedom, independence, and against the wickedness of certain powers inspired by the spirit of evil. Buddhism fights against inertia, listlessness, injustice. However, it respects other religions according to the teaching of King Asoka: 'Do not decry other sects, nor deprecate them, but on the contrary honor what is honorable in them.' "

Elsewhere Sihanouk states: "Buddhism is socialist in that it fights against evil and social injustice. Buddha did not give up that fight during the period of his life following his Illumination. He fought against dishonesty, theft, deceit, and lies, as well as the privileges the Brahmin caste considered its right. Buddhism is also a combat against all forms of suffering. . . . This temporal and dynamic aspect of Buddhism is expressed, finally, in man's will to go beyond himself, in his personal search for truth, as well as his sacrifices to help his fellow man, and in this form Buddhism is the finest ideal which could inspire our socialism."[1]

Jean Lacouture comments: "Thus Buddhism represents more than the too-often-cited call to 'Nirvana' (a supreme awakening as well as the achievement of serenity, in any case the ideal target of an active trajectory); it is a doctrine of individual responsibility, a summons to 'good

1 Philippe Peschez: *Essai sur la démocratie cambodienne.*

works.' Taking this interpretation to its limits, Sihanouk has made it a sort of centripetal and effervescent activism."[2]

The second constant we can discern in Sihanouk's praxis is the rejection of violence, of external constraints. Aware of, almost obsessed with, the Khmer people's numerical inferiority (five to seven million, compared to fifty million Vietnamese), he deliberately turned his back on centuries of violence and bloody confrontations. From Geneva in 1954, through the great conferences at Bandung, Belgrade, through all of his official visits to foreign countries, Sihanouk had a single object in mind: peace for his country, and an equilibrium he knew to be precarious. But even at the most difficult moments, and again in this book, he has never despaired of peace. One wonders why he has never been a Nobel laureate.

In Brioni, Yugoslavia, where he was the guest of Marshal Tito in 1973, he told the Italian journalist Oriana Fallaci: "Here I am completely immersed in a war, while I cannot abide war, weapons, uniforms, medals, explosions, bloodshed, death. I am so antimilitary that when I became King and had to take courses at a military academy, I could barely tell the difference between a sergeant and a captain. When the Vietminh came into Cambodia in 1953 on the claim that they would drive the French out, I got rid of them without firing a shot. All I said to them was; 'What the devil are you doing here? Get out!' Last year, a North Korean marshal said to me: 'The main reason your chief of staff overthrew you was that you do not directly oversee your army.' I answered him: 'You are a career soldier.

2 *Quatre hommes et leurs peuples,* Editions du Seuil.

That is your vocation. I am an artist. I was born
an artist and what I like best is the cinema, music, litera-
ture. . . ."

It is a fact that during Sihanouk's regime the ranks of
the Cambodian army were never more than 35,000. It was
not at all a comic-opera army, as it has sometimes been
described; it was rather a national security corps suited to
mixing with the people and also helping them with the daily
work of building the nation.

Norodom Sihanouk has always expressed the regret
that the International Control Commission set up by the
Geneva Conference in 1954 was totally without concrete
means to accomplish its mission, that it became no more
than an observation unit.

One of the major concerns of this book, finally, is to
demonstrate the absurdity of any attempts to solve Indochinese problems by forcible means. This is what separates
Prince Sihanouk fundamentally and in every respect from
a Lon Nol or a Pol Pot. He has always shown himself to be
a partisan of a negotiated peace with Vietnam. Not peace
at any price, of course, but with international guarantees.
What he always feared was a catastrophe caused by a
direct confrontation with Vietnam. One of the subjects of
his dispute with General Lon Nol in January to March,
1970, was additional troops to stand up to "Vietnamese
infiltration." Sihanouk refused. Lon Nol had dreams of
glory. Usually taciturn, one day he told me that if Norodom
Sihanouk (then head of state) gave him the wherewithal,
the Khmer army, with the help of the Americans, would
push "as far as the Point of Camau," the extreme southern
tip of Cochin China (a part of southern Vietnam that includes Ho Chi Minh city). He added "Furthermore, we
would have the complete support of a million Khmer Krom

in Cochin China; we could make quick work of recapturing that lost province of ours."

Lon Nol traded his dream (foiled by Norodom Sihanouk) for reality. The Prince was overthrown; the former chief of staff could give his ambitions free rein. What did Lon Nol do? With the blessing of President Nixon and the Pentagon and CIA hawks, he began by sending young people to smash the North and South Vietnamese embassies. Then he began to run down, mercilessly to decimate the some 400,000 ethnic Vietnamese living in Cambodia. The Mekong River was strewn with their water-swollen corpses. At the same time, the North Vietnamese and Vietcong with vanguard troops in a few mobile camps along the Vietnam-Cambodia border (the camps were really a backup base for the Vietcong troops fleeing the American army's massive search-and-destroy missions) were infiltrating Cambodia in huge numbers.

And what did Lon Nol do then? He called for help to his South Vietnamese and pro-American ally Nguyen Cao Ky. South Vietnamese and American troops went deep into Khmer territory and dedicated themselves to systematic searches, pillage, and rape on a large scale. As for the Khmer Krom, the South Vietnamese Cambodians, they turned up with Son Ngoc Thanh, well-trained and equipped by the CIA. They skimmed off the cream of Phnom Penh's capital, and acted like perfect warlords.

In the end Lon Nol the Conquerer, Lon Nol who wanted to subjugate Vietnam, was caught in the trap of his own making and placed at the mercy of the Vietnamese, with the pro-Americans on one side, the Vietminh on the other.

Strangely enough, starting in 1972 Pol Pot took the same erroneous course. It proved his undoing.

In this book, Norodom Sihanouk relates the bloody episodes punctuating the fratricidal power struggle of 1970 to 1975, between the Vietnamese in Hanoi, the Khmer Vietminh, and the Khmer Rouge—a struggle which appears to have taken precedence at times over the combat against the common enemy, "American imperialism."

Pol Pot, with his accomplice Ieng Sary (who was, however, also of South Vietnamese descent) made abundant use of Chinese aid (just as Lon Nol sought to use the United States) to launch a ferocious fight "against the hereditary Vietnamese enemy" (pejoratively called the Yuon), taking them violently to task in scornful, even insulting terms, driving Vietcong and Vietminh troops well beyond the Cambodian border, so far, the *yotheas* (Pol Pot's troops) said at the time, that "we could see sugar palms."

At the beginning, the Vietnamese responded to the provocation in January, 1978, with a vigorous military effort, but one temporally and physically limited. Pol Pot proclaimed victory, all too soon. The effort in question was essentially aimed at "liberating" and leading toward Vietnam some 150,000 Khmers, who were then inducted, trained, armed, and served as raw material for a second effort one year later, almost to the day.

What happened next is well known. Vietnam, pressing its overwhelming military advantage, pushed toward Phnom Penh. Instead of putting old Khmer Vietminh cadres in charge of the capital (the leftovers of the contingent taking refuge in Hanoi in 1954, after the Geneva agreements), the Vietnamese were smart enough to use Khmer Rouge dissidents, former close associates of Pol Pot's who had "rallied" to the Vietnamese cause.

But then what? Did that take care of the problem? Heng Samrin and his men, Norodom Sihanouk states, had been Pol Pot loyalists at one time. They too had blood on their hands, they too had taken part in the pogrom following the "liberation" of Phnom Penh in April, 1975, and the subsequent forced and furious collectivization; they did not make the least move against it. For the time being the Vietnamese, wanting to differentiate themselves from the Pol Pot regime, have supposedly adopted a more humane policy toward Cambodian people. But for how long? Heng Samrin will have to face the harsh reality of an insurrection, passive or active, by a people traditionally hostile to Vietnamese presence in their country. He will be forced to enter into the cycle of repression. Not to mention severe and pressing economic problems: because of the war effort, no rice has been planted in Cambodia this year; existing stocks have been "repatriated" to Vietnam. Heng Samrin will not be able to bridge the gap unless he receives massive aid from outside.

Is there a solution to Cambodia's problems? If Vietnam continues to support Heng Samrin, and China does the same for Pol Pot's guerrillas, there will be no alternative but to let them fight to the limit of their respective strength, Norodom Sihanouk thinks. Meanwhile, the majority of the population, people who have nothing to do with the fighting, will have to resort to fleeing the country.

Unless . . . unless the powers this conflict directly concerns—the People's Republic of China, the USSR, the member countries of ASEAN, including Thailand—sit down to negotiate, recognizing that an armed conflict would carry serious risks, could spread, besides the fact it could come to no satisfactory resolution.

Working from this hypothesis, a new Geneva Conference could determine the terms of withdrawal for the troops involved, reactivate the former International Control Commission, this time giving it the power to accomplish its mission on the spot through the active collaboration of armed contingents sent by Cambodia's "friends." It would restore internal peace, begin organizing for free and democratic elections. These elections would be monitored with international control, and all political parties (those of Lon Nol, Pol Pot, Heng Samrin, and any others) would be represented, including Prince Sihanouk, who, were he to win, would propose a mandate of four years.

Is this hypothesis unrealistic? Norodom Sihanouk is used to fighting against the odds. For nearly twenty years, he rowed against the current of his country's past, and against foreign influences.

Today the most serious commentators in London and Washington, from the English journalist William Shawcross to the former American Secretary of State Henry Kissinger, take a slightly different tack in considering Norodom Sihanouk's fall from power in 1967 through 1970. Until now there have only been studies of the former Cambodian head of state's "mistakes" in management or errors in judgment, the "corruption" of his court, the weakness of his regime, etc. But beyond these too often subjective judgments, another kind of analysis ought to be made. It would examine point by point the true influence of outside pressure on the regime, whether communist or Western. That was the real cause of the fall of a man and a government that obviously were and still are popular.

From here on in, let us view the actions of the various parties involved more dispassionately. The hour of truth has arrived.

The regime of exacerbated economic liberalism, the American-style republic instituted by Lon Nol, Sirik Matak, and Son Ngoc Thanh, has seen its day. A western import, it could concern only a few thousand people in Cambodia directly. The masses got nothing out of it. In the context of insurrection, it only hastened the break between the former kingdom and the two tiny minority opposition groups: the Communists on one side and the pro-Americans on the other. The Vietnamese, in Saigon as well as Hanoi, proceeded to slice up the country only Norodom Sihanouk's presence in power had kept intact.

To stand up to the crises of the Vietnam war, Sihanouk had two important advantages: his great popularity within the country and the trust certain other nations placed in him. Their trust was not misplaced; Sihanouk always tried to keep the peace.

Lon Nol, however, firmly believed in shows of force, in a war he had never had the means to wage. The Cambodian army was divided and reduced to its core when a majority of its members joined the *maquis;* then it was worn out by years of heavy fighting, in spite of massive drafting and the institution of martial law; it was undermined by the corruption and incompetence of its own most notorious chiefs. Thus it was in no condition to face 600,000 war-hardened, disciplined, incorruptible soldiers from Hanoi and from South Vietnam.

Furthermore, Saigon quickly imposed its terms and started acting like a conqueror. And to top things off, Lon Nol had banked too heavily on U.S. aid. He seized power just when the America's dearest wish was to find a *modus vivendi* permitting an "honorable" retreat from Southeast Asia.

As concerns the Khmer Vietminh, they were never able to gain a real foothold. Their cadres had lived and worked in Hanoi since 1954. They were probably too old and had probably begun to think like exiles. They were not welcomed by the Khmer Kandal—the plains Khmers—just as Phnom Penh's inhabitants were not fond of the Khmer Krom *tonton macoutes* that Son Ngoc Thanh brought back with him from South Vietnam. Furthermore, they underestimated how much pressure the Khmer Rouge cadres could put on ordinary people; for several years the cadres had been in the field, cleverly playing on old historical grudges of the minority population in Cambodia's high plateaus (the Khmer Loeus). This was a fairly nomadic population, planting burnbeat fields (in Ratanakiri, Mondolkiri), or picking cardamom pods (in Pursat, Koh Kong, Kompong Speu, Kampot). They envied the much more prosperous inhabitants of the plains (Khmer Kandal). The people of the high plateaus were much sought after, much worked on by special services of every variety; they formed the pool from which the Khmer Rouge found its future cadres. They were uneducated cadres, used to moving around, instructed in hatred. They behaved like brutes.

The Khmer Rouge thought that by killing off or deporting the inhabitants of the "bourgeois" towns, supposedly the strongholds of the republican regime, by instituting a Stalin-style dictatorship, by elimating all human and material reminders, direct or indirect, of the banished past, they would be able to ready the mold for a new, collectivized society. By barreling ahead, they no doubt hoped to move directly, with no transition, from Sirik Matak's flamboyant brand of capitalism into an Albanian-style Communism, with Pol Pot as its hero and uncontested leader.

This might have worked for a while on a tranquil island sheltered from any outside meddling. Unfortunately for Pol Pot, the neighboring Vietnamese were on the alert. Hanoi could not tolerate a Phnom Penh regime allied to China, an enemy to its southern neighbors. Pol Pot's regime collapsed not only because of its scorn for human life, but also because of bad blood between Cambodia and Vietnam.

Since not only the pro-American "Free" Khmer foundered, but also the pro-Vietnamese Khmer Vietminh and the pro-Chinese Khmer Rouge—at the price of more than 2,-300,000 dead and missing (800,000 under Lon Nol, 1,500,-000 under Pol Pot, not counting the victims of the current regime) and a country in ruins, back in the Stone Age or very near it, stripped of all its cadres and technicians—what is left for the Cambodian people? What recourse do they now have, if not to a man who always remained above factional fighting, who refused to fly different colors with every shift in the political wind?

At the age of fifty-six, after five years of exile and three of forced retirement, Norodom Sihanouk has only one ambition: to serve his country once more. But not on just any terms. He is and always has been his own man politically, even when he had to treat temporarily with his former adversaries the better to counter his new enemies. He is tired of the role of scapegoat, whether for left- or right-wing interests. He would institute the most democratic regime possible.

He is starting from scratch. His personal wealth is gone. He donated nearly all of his fortune to the Cambodian nation in 1963. The rest was taken from him by the Republican regime in 1970. At that time, he came into the equivalent of $20,000 in stock and currency from his mother, Queen Kossamak. A third party deposited it in a foreign bank. As soon as he could recover this sum in March, 1979, Prince Sihanouk immediately had it given to help Cambodian refugees in Thailand.

Since 1970, most of his personal expenses have been underwritten by the People's Republic of China. It would be easy enough to deduce that he is therefore at the mercy of the Chinese government. Sihanouk's gently humorous retort is that no one takes exception to the fact that De Gaulle took refuge in London in 1940; did that mean he acted as a subject of the King of England? Historically, China has been a faithful ally of Cambodia's; more recently, the terms of the Sino-Khmer joint declaration of October 3, 1964, have never been broken or reneged on: "China assures it will work tirelessly to strengthen Sino-Khmer friendship and will never betray the confidence Cambodia has placed in it."

From 1976 to 1978, Sihanouk's daily fare was brought to him by his Khmer Rouge jailers in Phnom Penh. "At one time they stopped coming for several days. My wife Monique and I thought we were going to starve to death," he said later. There was a story at the time that he was made to grow his own food in a garden. A story like so many others about Norodom Sihanouk.

The truth is that Norodom Sihanouk provokes comment. If it is reported he likes *foie gras,* or plays the saxophone, or composes songs, witticisms abound. But no one takes exception to the fact Edward Heath has conducted an orchestra, or Valéry Giscard d'Estaing has played his accordion in public . . .

Sihanouk's policy of neutrality earned him the nickname "the weathervane prince." But now when the wind shifts in Cambodia it stirs up bloodstained soil. And today, no one laughs in Cambodia.

There is not now a single Cambodian able to speak out who does not miss "the good old Sangkum days." Would things have turned out differently if Cambodia had put up a united front when the country was threatened from two sides in 1970? If they had stuck together, it would have made resistance easier, invasion more difficult. But history cannot be rewritten.

This is no time for regrets. Realism and common sense must prevail. They dictate that everything must be done to help the Cambodian people recover their freedom and independence as quickly as possible. They must be given the means, with international guarantees and supervision, to choose the political regime they desire.

In the sweepstakes for peace, Norodom Sihanouk is a heavy favorite.

INTRODUCTION
BY WILLIAM SHAWCROSS

The 1970s were the decade in which Cambodia died. It was not an act of God, but a man-made disaster, and it continues today. Eventually the destruction of Cambodia will be recognized as one of the great crimes of the twentieth century. But unlike the crimes of the Third Reich, it does not seem possible that the crucial evidence will ever be gathered all in one place so that a complete and coherent history can be easily assembled. The truth will have to be pieced together slowly, step by step, little by little. Norodom Sihanouk's memoirs and views are an essential, if not conclusive, part of that process.

Ten years ago Cambodia was a self-sufficient agricultural nation of some seven million people, the vast majority of whom lived peacefully in their villages. Throughout the fifties and sixties, Sihanouk had presided feudally over the nation, and had largely succeeded in his main ambition: to keep Cambodia out of the war that was taking place in the neighboring and traditionally antagonistic country of Vietnam. But in March, 1970, during a visit abroad, Sihanouk was overthrown in a bloodless coup. At once the little state careered off the narrow "neutral" course along which he had tried to steer it and headed toward annihilation.

One can divide the seventies into roughly three periods: first, the war. From Sihanouk's overthrow till April, 1975, the nation was overturned. His usurper, General Lon Nol, attempted, with the support of the White house and in particular of Richard Nixon and Henry Kissinger, to defeat the Vietnamese. For five years the White House sustained Lon Nol's futile and vainglorious efforts—and Cambodian society was uprooted in the process. Over half the seven million inhabitants fled from their villages to the towns, where they became totally dependent upon American food aid. At first many refugees said they were fleeing the American and South Vietnamese bombing that spread across the country after 1970, but increasingly their reasons emphasized their desire to escape the cruelty of the Khmer Rouge. This was a resistance movement that had scarcely existed at the beginning of 1970 except as a tiny *maquis* group with no hope of seizing power—but one that fed upon the entrails of war.

The second period was revolution, a revolution so atrocious that it still defies explanation. As soon as the Khmer Rouge defeated the exhausted government and the army of Lon Nol in April, 1975, they drove the refugees and indigenous townspeople back into the countryside. The towns were emptied completely; Cambodia was to begin again at "Year Zero." The old society, which was certainly rigidly hierarchical and corrupt, was to be swept away. All its traces and all its people were to be eliminated. For the next four years the Khmer Rouge leaders, a tiny band ("The Pol Pot–Ieng Sary clique") of about half-a-dozen men and women, most of whom were related, attempted to create a new society based upon collective agriculture. No one knows how many people died under their regime, but the estimates go as high as three million. Even if that is an exaggeration, there is no doubt that the death toll was monstrous. All those associated with the *ancien règime*— soldiers, policemen, civil servants, teachers—risked execution. So did their families. Doctors, engineers, lawyers—all those thought to be middle class or intellectual—were also in peril. For those who escaped execution, which often took the form of an axe handle in the back of the neck, death came more slowly. The Khmer Rouge refused to allow the use of Western medicine and food was always scarce. Yet they imposed draconian work regimes in the fields. Hundreds of thousands of people, young and old especially, collapsed from sickness and exhaustion.

The third period continues today: it includes occupation and the looming threat of famine. The Khmer Rouge policy toward Hanoi had been one of belligerent hostility. They conducted border raids into Vietnam, treating Vietnamese villagers with as much contempt as their own people. In January, 1979, the Vietnamese army invaded, captured Phnom Penh within a week, and sent the Khmer Rouge fleeing back into the mountains and jungles from whence they had emerged only four years before. Since then the Vietnamese have fought to eliminate the Khmer Rouge. By the beginning of 1980 they had not succeeded, and new resistance groups, some of them pledging allegiance to Sihanouk, had sprung up in the western part of the country.

The continued fighting through 1979 and 1980, and the fact that the Vietnamese allowed people to return from the work camps built by the Khmer Rouge to their former homes, meant that very little of the main 1979 rice crop was planted. At the same time, around half a million Cambodians fled the fighting for the relative sanctuary of the Thailand border, where they sat listlessly in refugee camps destined, perhaps, to become new "Palestinians," pawns in the great power struggles in which Cambodia had been caught.

Through the second half of 1979 food was shipped into Cambodia from the West, amid conflicting reports that the Vietnamese and their client government were now being uncooperative, and charges that the international relief agencies were being dilatory. At the beginning of 1980 it seemed that the worst threat of famine had been averted, but it was clear that the earliest the country could possibly return to rice self-sufficiency was 1981. Massive international aid was essential, at least until that time.

Journalists and relief workers who visited Cambodia during 1979–1980 were struck by the terrible emptiness of the country and the desolation of the survivors. The nation had lost its sinews and its spirit. The towns and cities were still largely derelict; hardly any members of the educational class could be traced, and families, as such, barely existed. Everyone had tales of how brothers, sisters, husbands, wives, children, and parents had perished under the Khmer Rouge. Whether and how an independent, functioning society could ever be rebuilt on this wreckage was very hard to say. There was no precedent for Cambodia. Never before had a revolution, however ruthless, practised what had become known as "auto-genocide."

In this book Sihanouk, who is now in exile in the West and who hopes still to play a part in his country's life, gives us his views on what has happened. The book is truly Sihanouk: astute, witty, opinionated, bombastic, and consistent only in one fundamental sense—it expresses his overriding interest in Cambodia.

It is part of Cambodia's misfortune that it was always difficult for Western (and Soviet) officials to take Sihanouk seriously. His high-pitched voice, his bragging, his consuming obsession with his talents as a film maker and a musician (while he was still in power in the sixties), all combined to make him an easy figure of fun. Yet just as Tito forged the independence of Yugoslavia and Nehru incarnated India, so Sihanouk built, and in a real sense personified, Cambodia. He made terrible errors in the sixties; like other leaders elsewhere he paid far too little attention to domestic politics and concerns, and it was this that brought about

his undoing. But his foreign policy, which consisted of playing the United States off against Hanoi in order to try and
prevent the Vietnam war from engulfing his country, was
for the most part successful. In *War and Hope* he takes
on some of his critics. The Lon Nol and Khmer Rouge
governments, he points out, shared the same fatal illu-
sions: that a country of seven million, underarmed, could
provoke and defeat a hostile neighbor with a population of
some 50 million:

> Lon Nol the super-believer, and Pol Pot, the super-
> atheist, agreed on at least one point: they thought
> they were better than Napoleon or Hitler. They
> thought it was impossible for their anti-Vietnamese
> campaign to end up like Waterloo or Stalingrad . . .
> But what has the final result of their anti-Vietnam
> campaign been?
>
> Today Cambodia is no more than a shambles. The
> Kampuchean people have been dismembered,
> crushed by the unbearable weight of an endless war
> a few foreign powers are keeping alive . . . until the
> last Kampuchean is dead.

Sihanouk's own tactics were very different. Throughout the sixties his policy of inglorious compromise led him
to allow the Vietnamese Communists to establish base
camps across the border from South Vietnam and to truck
supplies from the deepwater port of Sihanoukville. He also
turned a blind eye to American hit-and-run attacks on the
base camps—all in the interests of keeping the war
confined to the border areas. Such compromise earned him
the understandable hostility of American military commanders, but Lyndon Johnson always refused military
requests that he permit a full-scale assault upon the sanc-

tuaries, mindful of the consequences this could have upon Cambodia itself. Richard Nixon and Henry Kissinger, however, threw such caution to the winds.

In his own memoirs Kissinger defends first the secret 1969–1970 bombing of the sanctuaries (which was carried out without the advice and consent of Congress), and then the U.S. invasion of 1970 on the grounds that Hanoi had violated Cambodia's neutrality first, and that a neutral nation has a duty to prevent its territory being abused by a belligerent in a war. This is true, but at the same time the practice of the two world wars suggests that a small neutral state is not at fault when it fails to resist the invasion of its territory, especially if such resistance would clearly not only be hopeless but also destructive of the state. Sihanouk was quite convinced that this was the case; the cataclysm brought about by his successors' attempts to defeat Vietnam proved him right.

Sihanouk spent most of the seventies with or representing the Khmer Rouge. From 1970–1975 he was their figurehead leader in Peking. They exploited his name to rally peasant support, but never had the slightest intention of allowing him real power. It was not until he returned home after their victory in 1975 that he realized the true nature of the regime he had been supporting. Yet even then he was kept in ignorance of what was really happening in his country. For three years he was detained under house arrest in the empty city of Phnom Penh, with only the Voice of America and the BBC to supply him with news. He was flown first to Peking and then to New York by the Chinese when Vietnam invaded at the end of 1978, and since then has been arguing Cambodia's case from Peking, North Korea, and the West.

I saw him in January, 1979, at the United Nations. He was categorical about where the responsibility for Cambodia's demise really lay. No one country could be blamed, he said. "There are only two men responsible for the tragedy in Cambodia today: Mr. Nixon and Dr. Kissinger. Lon Nol was nothing without them and the Khmer Rouge were nothing without Lon Nol. Mr. Nixon and Dr. Kissinger gave the Khmer Rouge involuntary aid because the people had to support the Communist patriots against Lon Nol. By expanding the war into Cambodia Nixon and Kissinger killed a lot of Americans and many other people; they spent enormous sums of money—four billion dollars—and the results were the opposite of what they wanted. They demoralized America, they lost all of Indochina to the Communists, and they created the Khmer Rouge."

In this book, however, Sihanouk is much more cautious in his criticism of the United States. His central argument is that if Cambodia is to be saved, a new international conference—like that held in Geneva in 1954—must be called. For that American support is essential. Moreover, Kissinger visited Sihanouk in Peking in April, 1979, to try and get him to accept the Kissinger version of Cambodia's history. Sihanouk would not agree with Kissinger's repeated assertion that he never wanted Lon Nol and always hoped that Sihanouk would return. The Prince said that if Kissinger finally wanted to be friends, that was fine; he would let bygones be bygones.

This is a fairly typical Sihanouk gesture. His only real consistency has always been his ambition to conserve Cambodia—and to this end almost any expediency has been justified. That he has made serious errors cannot be denied. In the sixties he was negligent about the discontent seething at home. In the seventies he was too quick after his overthrow to join his former enemy, the Khmer Rouge, and, with his name, give them instant and widespread legitimacy at home. At that time, however, the Khmer Rouge were a tiny group with no great reputation for brutality, and Sihanouk's decision reflected his conviction that the United States had encouraged, if not inspired, Lon Nol's coup d'état and was now determined to involve Cambodia fully in its Vietnam effort. This was close to the truth. But, for the moment, Sihanouk feels that the only hope of any salvation for the remains of Cambodia lies in a compromise involving the super-powers and all the countries of the region. In order to achieve this he is seeking support everywhere, even from old enemies like Kissinger.

The problems involved in recalling the 1954 Geneva Conference, or in constituting any other such international body, are immense. Apart from anything else, in 1954 the USSR and China were allied in their defence of Hanoi; now their enmity is one of the principal causes of warfare in that region. Vietnam, the ally of Moscow, has said that the situation in Cambodia is "irreversible," while China, the ally of the Khmer Rouge, has said that it is "intolerable." But without some such compromise, the tensions in the whole of Indochina, and therefore in much of Southeast Asia, will remain insupportable for the peoples there, and Cambodia will remain the cockpit of war. In 1970 the population was around seven million; today it is thought to be between four and five million. If the Cambodian people are to be abused by outside powers in the eighties as they were abused in the seventies by both foreigners and their own people, by the end of this coming decade there may be none left at all. When one considers Sihanouk and his suggestions today, it is well to remember that in the refugee camps in Thailand it is common to hear people say that they will never return to Cambodia under the Vietnamese nor under the Khmer Rouge, but only under Sihanouk. His was not a golden age, but it was the only age of peace. He deserves credit.

WAR AND HOPE

THE CASE FOR CAMBODIA

BIRTH OF A CONFLICT

1 Zbigniew Brzezinski, the head of President Jimmy Carter's National Security Council, has asserted that the Vietnamese-Cambodian war is nothing but a violent manifestation of the rivalry and international power struggle between the two Communist giants, Russia and China: he called it "a war by proxy." His statement corresponds to one segment of reality. Specialists on Asia and Indochina always stress the fact that from time immemorial the Vietnamese and the Khmers have been mortal enemies, and that Vietnam, the much stronger nation, has always tended to swallow up Khmer land.

That is still true. But other, very important factors also enter into the dispute between Communist Vietnam and Pol Pot's self-styled "Democratic" Kampuchea. These factors are the following:

—the many differences between the Khmer converted to Communism by the North Vietnamese (Ho Chi Minh), whom I call the "Khmer Vietminh," and the "Khmer Rouge," that is, Khmers who became Communists as students in French universities and later developed into Maoist extremists;

—the accumulation of incidents and ill will between the North Vietnamese and the Khmer Rouge within Cambodia between 1955 and 1959, from 1970 (the year of Lon Nol's anti-Sihanouk coup d'état) to 1975, and from 1975 (the year of the Khmer Rouge victory in Phnom Penh and of the North Vietnamese in Saigon) through 1978;

—the Khmer Rouge's supernationalism and their visceral "nostalgia" for "Kampuchea Krom";

—the fact that the Khmer Rouge had to compensate

for their tremendous errors in domestic policy by deliberately diverting the people's attention toward the "Vietnamese threat";

—the Khmer Rouge's erroneous and catastrophic belief in their own military superiority;

—the deadly lessons in cruelty the Khmer Rouge leaders gave their soldiers and political commissars;

—the fact that the North Vietnamese were too intelligent to miss the chance to take over Democratic Kampuchea when the Khmer Rouge offered it to them on a silver platter;

—finally, the Soviets' opportunism and double revenge on the Khmer Rouge, who scornfully rejected all their advances and those of their Eastern European satellites between 1974 and 1977, and on the People's Republic of China. China's huge success in Romania and Yugoslavia (Hua Guofeng's state visit in 1978, the statements—so humiliating for the Russians—Romanian, and Yugoslavian leaders made on that occasion), its success with Japan (a peace-and-friendship treaty signed in 1978) and with the United States (the establishment of full diplomatic relations between China and the U.S. on January 1, 1979, the recent and remarkable "honeymoon" in Sino-American relations): all this has pushed the Russians toward a vendetta. Democratic Kampuchea is paying for it.

In the following chapters my readers will find these factors further described, as each one warrants.

KHMER VIETMINH AND
KHMER ROUGE

Much in the same way that there are two types of Communism (Chinese and Soviet) opposing each other on an international level, Cambodia, too, has two bitterly competitive types of Communism: the Khmer Vietminh and the Khmer Rouge.

The Khmer Vietminh, the older group, came into prominence during the First Indochinese War, which pitted Ho Chi Minh's Communists against the return of French colonialism. Between 1947 and 1954, Ho Chi Minh's North Vietnamese (called the Vietminh) strove to create a secondary front in Cambodia, and consequently to launch an auxiliary insurrectionist movement among the Cambodians. The overwhelming majority of Khmer were dedicated royalists and Buddhists, so the Vietnamese were able to turn only a tiny minority into Communists (about five thousand full-fledged members in 1954).

At the first Geneva Conference on Indochina (July, 1954), the joint efforts of the People's Republic of China, the Soviet Union, and Ho Chi Minh's government to have the Khmer Vietminh designated a liberated zone within Cambodia, patterned on Laos's Pathet Lao liberated zone, came to nothing.

The first Khmer Vietminh setback: the Royal Crusade for Cambodia's independence had reached a successful conclusion in November, 1953, some three months before the Geneva Conference, when France signed over the final powers (including military power) to the royal government, then headed by His Excellency Penn Nouth.

The second setback: the Kingdom of Cambodia was the only Indochinese state to emerge intact from the Geneva Conference, that is, with no granting of a partition to the Communists.

Number three: in the general legislative elections of 1955, which took place under international control (India, Poland, Canada), the Pracheachon party (the Vietminh's party) won only 3 percent of the vote and not one seat in the Khmer parliament.

Pol Pot, in the endless speeches he gave in Phnom Penh in 1977 and 1978, strongly reprimanded the Khmer Vietminh and their Hanoi superiors for these "unforgivable" Communist defeats. He stressed the need for a new and authentic Kampuchean Communist Party—his own, "the only one able" to overthrow feudalism (i.e., the monarchy) and lead the country to "true independence and sovereignty."

What do we know about Pol Pot and his party? First of all, Khmer Rouge leaders belong to two categories of intellectuals:

The members of the first category—I call them "the Superintellectuals"—have advanced degrees. Khieu Samphan, for example, won a doctorate in economics from a famous French university. Thiounn Mumm is the only Khmer ever to graduate from France's École Polytechnique. The two other specimens, now internationally famous, were Hou Yuon and Hu Nim, both doctors of law. Hou Yuon, Minister of the Interior, and Hu Nim, Minister of Propaganda, were most probably assassinated (one just after the victory of April 17, 1975, the other in late March or early April, 1977) on the orders of Pol Pot and Ieng Sary, who did not relish being unfavorably compared to the two dynamic and popular ministers.

The members of the second category are former elementary teachers who became "professors" after taking teacher-training courses in France (Ieng Sary, for instance), or else high-school teachers (like Son Sen).

What these two categories of Khmer Rouge had in common was their hatred of the monarchy ("Two thousand years is too long," their slogan ran); a supernationalism much more chauvinistic than Sihanouk's; a passionate love for the People's Republic of China and a boundless admiration for Chinese Communism in its most extreme and terrible form (the Cultural Revolution). And yet these Khmer Rouge leaders had started out as nationalist republicans, supporters of Son Ngoc Thanh, when they were students or schoolteachers.

During the 1940s Son Ngoc Thanh had appeared to be the champion of the fight against the French protectorate, against the Cambodian monarchy, and "for independence and democracy." In March, 1973, Hu Nim explained to me that he and his comrades had stopped supporting Thanh once they realized that he was not a patriot but "the vile agent of Japanese and American imperialism." Son Ngoc Thanh was really no more than an employee of the Tokyo government, and later of the CIA.

When they came in contact with French and international Communists during their student days, the young "antifeudalists" turned Red. They returned to Phnom Penh and after 1956 entered into relations with diplomats from the People's Republic of China; these Parisian Communists thus became Maoist Reds. Between 1956 and 1970 (the date of Lon Nol's coup d'état), the Khmer Rouge continued to grow and fill out ideologically, suckled by China. According to Pol Pot himself, more and more frequent contacts, a more and more fruitful collaboration, between the Peking embassy in Phnom Penh and the Khmer Rouge ringleaders were secretly and smoothly established. A good number of them were even able to make secret visits to Mao Zedong in China. The five years of war against the Americans and Lon Nol (1970–1975) only strengthened the love knot binding Khmer Rouge leaders to their Peking counterparts.

Ironically, it was the Vietnamese Communists who were assigned the role of cuckold in this rather unusual affair. Witness the many Khmer Rouge trips (Kampuchea–China, China–Kampuchea) that had to be organized by the Hanoi government, since the route was essentially straight across Vietnam.

Furthermore, when the Khmer Rouge leaders in Phnom Penh decided to "flee Sihanouk," to join the *maquis*, some in the 1950s, others in the 1960s, they enjoyed the ready-made bases and protection their North Vietnamese and Vietcong colleagues offered them in certain frontier regions of the Khmer kingdom, infested by their Red neighbors.

A Radio Hanoi program in December, 1978, claimed the Khmer Rouge had subsequently poisoned the old and ailing Son Ngoc Minh with an eye to taking over the leadership of the united Khmer Communist movement, that is, uniting the Khmer Rouge and Khmer Vietminh.

The Hanoi Government made a similar unification effort just after Lon Nol's coup d'état (March 18, 1970), since it then hastened to repatriate the five thousand political cadres and Khmer Vietminh officers who had been trained in Vietnam.

Two years ago (1978), during a car trip my wife and I made with him through a Khmer province, President of the Presidium Khieu Samphan confirmed this massive repatriation and declared that the cadres and officers involved were "no longer Khmers in their hearts or minds," that they had become "Vietminh spies" and that consquently (I quote) "We [the Khmer Rouge] had to get rid of them." This simply meant that the Khmer Vietminh reinforcement Hanoi had sent in 1970 to help us in our fight against the Americans ended up being liquidated (physically) by the Khmer Rouge.

Khieu Samphan also confirmed that there had been violent confrontations between Khmer Rouge units and Vietminh and Vietcong troops, even though Cambodia was in the middle of a war against the U.S. and Lon Nol. In my opinion this delayed our common victory over the common enemy by several years.

ANTI-VIETMINH ACCUSATIONS AND RESENTMENT

During my one-month stay (March, 1973) in the liberated zone during the anti-U.S. and anti–Lon Nol war, the Khmer Rouge leaders (Khieu Samphan, Hu Nim, Son Sen) frequently spoke to me about the "serious offenses" committed by the North Vietnamese in Kampuchea. Among the more or less credible offenses they mentioned were:

—the rape of Khmer women or girls and murders of patriots or peasants refusing to serve the Vietnamese Communists' interests, whatever form they took;

—thefts from the Khmers who sheltered the Vietnamese; the "visitors" took carts, bicycles, wristwatches, etc;

—abusive purchases of consumer goods, to the detriment of the Khmer Rouge's army service corps, forcing Pol Pot and his men to put an end to private trade, the free circulation of merchants and goods, of breeders and their livestock, in mid-1973; houses, villages, and their populations were then regrouped into cooperatives (closely supervised by Khmer Rouge cadres);

—installation (by the Vietnamese) of military camps on bases "throughout sovereign Cambodian territory" and without the previous authorization of the FUNK (National United Front of Kampuchea);

—the recruitment, despite the strict opposition of Khmer Rouge leaders, of Cambodian men and women as auxiliary fighters in the Vietnamese forces;

—deliberate sabotage of the development of the Khmer Rouge armed forces and their progress in combat; the slowing of military and other aid from China to the

Khmer Rouge; impudent filching of Chinese trucks and jeeps, heavy arms, modern weapons, munitions, and other gifts sent from China for the Khmer Rouge;

—Vietnamese aggressions with the intention of destroying the Khmer Rouge's best units. Khieu Samphan and his comrades explained to me, regarding this, that the North Vietnamese desperately wanted to nip Khmer Rouge power in the bud so as to prepare for the coming to power (after a foreseeable victory over the U.S. and Lon Nol) of a government that would be Cambodian in appearance only and in reality Vietnam's servant.

My own thoughts on what was behind the conflict between the Khmer Rouge and the North Vietnamese are the following: Pol Pot, Ieng Sary, and Co. were so full of hatred for the Khmer monarchy and Norodom Sihanouk that they could not tolerate the triple blow the same monarchy and the same Sihanouk dealt to Hanoi and the Khmer Vietminh in 1953 (the royal crusade for Kampuchea's complete independence), 1954 (the Geneva Conference on Indochina), and 1955 (legislative elections in Cambodia). These three setbacks made the Khmer Rouge so furious they threw themselves irreversibly into Peking's arms and violently fought against those responsible for the inadmissible humiliation. Pol Pot's speeches leave no doubt as to this.

In March, 1973, Son Sen (Deputy Prime Minister and National Defense Minister in Pol Pot's government) revealed the following "historic" detail to me: before joining the *maquis*, he, Son Sen (then only a teacher), had a strange proposition one day from Gen. Lon Nol, "Sihanouk's right-hand man." During an audience, the general bluntly told him: "Your Khmer Rouge and my many partisans and I share a common goal. We both feel an unquenchable hatred for the Khmer monarchy and Norodom Sihanouk. Up to this point we have chosen and used two

11

different routes to an eventual elimination of these two abominable enemies. But they are rather powerful enemies. In order to be able to overthrow and replace them, it is indispensable for us to join forces and coordinate our plans, efforts, and action. I therefore propose a secret alliance to you." For my benefit and in the presence of his comrades (Pol Pot, Ieng Sary, Hu Nim, Hou Yuon, etc.), Son Sen concluded his story by saying: "We [the Khmer Rouge] categorically refused any such alliance and let Lon Nol's clique know that each camp must work separately."

The story is worth mentioning here because it gives the Khmer Rouge's position very clearly: they were hostile to Lon Nol's reactionary right-wingers, but Norodom Sihanouk, the inevitable and temporary ally, was still Enemy Number One, their "mark" . . . after the victory.

In his harangue (length: five hours!) on the seventeenth anniversary of the Communist Party of Kampuchea (September, 1977), Pol Pot bitterly denounced the North Vietnamese, with their sanctuaries in Kampuchea, for not helping the Khmer Rouge logistically and for being too indulgent with the "feudal power," that is, the royal government of Cambodia.

In fact the North Vietnamese had found themselves in a quandary after the Geneva Conference: on the one hand, as Communists they were duty-bound to help the Khmer Rouge to organize in the Cambodian *maquis*, and on the other hand they could not afford a falling out with Norodom Sihanouk. First of all, Sihanouk had closed his eyes to the installation of Viet "rest camps," hospitals, provision centers in Cambodia. Secondly, he authorized the Chinese, Russians, Czechoslovakians, etc., to use the port of Sihanoukville (Kompong Som) as an unloading point for the military and other supplies to the Vietminh and Vietcong. Thirdly, he officially supported the Vietnamese Communists' just cause on the international level; they were patriotically fighting against American imperialism, under very difficult conditions.

Pol Pot and his comrades had first of all chosen to establish their principal anti-Sihanouk guerrilla bases next to the Vietnamese sanctuaries in the provinces of Ratanakiri, Stung Treng, Mondolkiri, and Kratié, and in the districts of Memot (Kompong Cham), Koh Andet–Phnom Den (Takeo), Kompong Trach (Kampot), and Chantrea-Prasaut (Svay Rieng), all of which bordered on Vietnam. But the lax protection and very ambiguous support by the Vietnamese led the Khmer Rouge to split with their Ho Chi Minh–led comrades during the 1960s and to set up their bases far from the sanctuaries. That is how the Khmer Rouge leaders founded new guerrilla bases in the forests and mountains of Kompong Speu (Mount Aural, Cambodia's highest mountain, 5,948 feet tall), Kompong Thom, Kompong Chhnang, Prey Veng, Siem Reap, Battambang, Oddor Meanchey, Preah Vihear—the last four bordering on Thailand. During the 1950s, the Khmer Rouge numbered in the hundreds. During the 1960s, they were able to recruit a few thousand more *yothea*s (soldiers) and civilian members, as well as a few dozen intellectuals.

Then came March 18, 1970, the "historic" day of Lon Nol's coup d'état overthrowing Sihanouk. From that day on, the coolness that had formerly characterized relations between the Khmer Rouge and the Vietnamese changed into an overt struggle to control new recruits—or cannon fodder.

From Peking, Norodom Sihanouk launched his appeal to the Khmer people that they rise up, join the *maquis*, and begin an armed fight against the treacherous Lon Nol, Sirik Matak, and their masters, the American imperialists. Sihanouk specified that once they had formed a guerrilla army patriot volunteers would find friends ready to give them rifles and ammunition and furnish them with adequate military training.

While they were happy with Sihanouk's appeal to the Khmer people, the Khmer Rouge and the Vietnamese became mortal enemies, because on the one hand Pol Pot's followers categorically denied the Vietnamese the least right to take in the Khmer joining the *maquis* as a result of Lon Nol's unpopular and antinational coup; and on the other hand the Vietnamese went right ahead and openly competed with the Khmer Rouge for the fresh recruits. They were aware the great majority of the new guerrilla fighters were not about to become Communists, that quite to the contrary they were firm nationalists and Sihanouk supporters, so the Vietnamese enticed them to enlist with thundering pro-Sihanouk slogans and the "generous" distribution of badges with a picture of Samdech Euv ("Prince Father"), as the people called Sihanouk.

The Hanoi crowd had another trump in their hand: they could offer the new Khmer fighters very modern weapons and a wealth of ammunition, while the Khmer Rouge had only a very limited stock of outdated arms and often mismatched ammunition. The Sihanouk supporters taken in by the Vietnamese were quickly formed into strong units tightly controlled by Hanoi officers, while those who ended up with the Khmer Rouge were "desihanoukized" and "polpotized," willingly or not; any who resisted were put out of the way, without benefit of trial.

Mini-conferences between the Khmer Rouge and the Vietnamese later took place in both countries, in an effort to reconcile their differences and present a united front to Lon Nol and his American backers. The Cambodians and Vietnamese would work in unison; all Khmer Communist armed units would be united under the sole direction of the Khmer Rouge (Pol Pot and his followers were most vocal on that point).

According to Khieu Samphan, after bitter discussions the Vietnamese finally agreed to send the Khmer Rouge leaders the five thousand Khmer Vietminh cadres Hanoi had trained (between 1954 and 1970), as well as the pro-Sihanouk units Lon Nol's men called the Khmer Rumdoh (Liberation Khmers), trained by Vo Nguyen Giap's officers. The Khmer Vietminh cadres and the pro-Sihanouk units were "polpotized." Still, Khieu Samphan claims, most of them would not "listen to reason" and consequently had to be liquidated. Of course when Khieu Samphan told me about the unfortunate Sihanouk supporters eaten up by the machine of the bloody Khmer Rouge–Vietnamese rivalry, he was careful to refer to them as hooligans who had "sold themselves body and soul" to the "Yuons" (a pejorative term the Cambodians use to designate the North Vietnamese).

AN "EXTRAORDINARY" WAR, 1970–1975

During the five years of our joint fight against American imperialism, Saigon President Nguyen Van Thieu's army, and Lon Nol's "republic," I had the honor of visiting North Vietnam a dozen or so times. Each time I stayed in Hanoi I had the opportunity to speak at length, and I must admit cordially, with North Vietnam's principal leaders, particularly Pham Van Dong, Vo Nguyen Giap, Truong Chinh, Le Duan, Nguyen Duy Trinh, and even the very elderly, amiable, and lucid President Ton Duc Thang.

I had a particularly trusting and affectionate friendship with Pham Van Dong and Vo Nguyen Giap. They liked to come to my Hanoi residence and have lunch or dinner with me. Before and after the meal we would have long and informative conversations about current events, especially our joint anti-American undertaking.

It is true that we had a common language, French, and that Communists like Dong, Giap, Truong Chinh, etc., delighted in appearing very different from the classic Communist prototype. Even when they spoke to the international press, Pham Van Dong and his team wanted to appear as open and eloquent as the classic-style Communist is closed-minded and closed-mouthed.

Vo Nguyen Giap, the glorious victor of Dien Bien Phu, also took pleasure in organizing work sessions for me during which we discussed the best military strategy to adopt against our common enemies. These work sessions were very instructive to me, since they revealed that the North Vietnamese knew Kampuchea like the backs of their hands. Giap would exhibit extremely well-made ordnance survey maps; he introduced me to his Kampuchea-specialist staff colonels, who could point out on the maps smallest bodies of water still full during the dry season—with their eyes closed. Thus I could clearly see that the Vietnamese were leaving nothing to chance and would be extremely dangerous adversaries if we Cambodians were to challenge them, as Lon Nol had done beginning in March, 1970.

But how could we go about exorcising the age-old hatred pitting the Khmers against the "Yuons"? Even the FUNK ministers, when they were invited to Hanoi in 1970–1971, the best period of our alliance with North Vietnam, managed to speak in their Hanoi guesthouse about "the Yuons' hypocrisy" and the "need for the Khmers in the FUNK to beware of North Vietnam's desire for hegemony after our foreseeable joint victory over the Yankee agressors and the traitor Lon Nol."

And, since walls have ears, the FUNK ministers' qualms were repeated to General Giap. Shortly thereafter, his face flushed with anger, he expressed his indignation to me in the following terms: "We North Vietnamese are genuine Communists, men of our word. We promised you solemnly and in writing that we would always respect your sovereignty, your national independence, your territory as it now stands, including the coastal islands. We will never break our promises. The greatest proof of our loyalty to Kampuchea and its chief of state [myself, at that time] is the sacrifice of Vietnam's finest, hundreds of whom have already given their lives for your country. It is a serious insult for the FUNK ministers to lump us together, most unfairly, with the American imperialist aggressors of our three Indochinese countries. Their anti-Vietnamese remarks, made here in Hanoi, hurt us deeply, since every day our soldiers, far from their dear homeland and their beloved families, fight and die on the sacred soil of our Khmer brothers and sisters, side by side with them against our common enemies, to save and liberate your country, Kampuchea."

Though they did not realize it, luck was with Lon Nol and the Americans during that period. The Khmer Rouge and the Vietnamese quickly moved from verbal exchanges to trading fire. The pursuit of our joint effort was seriously handicapped as a result.

In March, 1973, my wife Monique and I were escorted from North Vietnam to the Laos-Cambodia border by our Vietnamese friends (including the Ambassador Nguyen Thuong) in Soviet-made jeeps, by way of one of the many Ho Chi Minh trails. We had barely arrived in Cambodia when Ambassador Nguyen Thuong whispered to Monique (while I was embracing Hu Nim and Son Sen) to ask me if I would please not speak in praise of the Democratic Republic of Vietnam and not say I was happy to have sealed the FUNK's alliance with his country. Why? "Because our Cambodian comrades are so touchy on the subject," he said. That was my first surprise regarding the state of relations between the Khmer Rouge and their Vietnamese comrades-at-arms.

During 1978, Khieu Samphan, my successor as Kampuchea's head of state, came out and told me that even in the midst of the anti-American war, the Cambodian Communist Party and revolutionary army had never stopped considering Vietnam and its army as Enemy Number One. He specified: "The Americans could conquer our country only superficially, while the Vietnamese would swallow it up, send millions of their citizens to colonize us, reducing our eight million Cambodians to an ethnic minority: it would be the end of our race and our national sovereignty!"[1]

That is no doubt one of the reasons Lon Nol's very weak Khmer Republic did not come tumbling down sooner. Even the American press, which in 1971–1972 predicted Lon Nol's fall for 1973 at the latest, was astounded by the regime's "inexplicable" longevity. The cause of this astonishing longevity was simple: the Khmer Rouge were not overly preoccupied with American imperialism. Their primary concern was to get even with their Vietminh and Vietcong comrades-at-arms, not to mention the laborious liquidation of the Khmer Vietminh and pro-Sihanouk forces! The war that lasted from March, 1970 until April, 1975 was truly an unusual, an extraordinary one.

1 When Khieu Samphan spoke about "eight million Cambodians," he was far from accurate: Cambodia's total population, even then, was no more than five million.

THE KHMER ROUGE AND NORTH VIETNAMESE KILL EACH OTHER OFF... AND WIN THE WAR AGAINST THE AMERICANS

One day in March, 1973, while I was in the liberated zone, I asked Son Sen (then the Khmer Rouge army chief of staff) how his troops and the Vietnamese managed to coordinate their war effort. Son Sen calmly replied that the Vietnamese "shifted for themselves." This means they were fighting separately, with no coordination, no mutual aid, no idea of what the other was doing against their very powerful American enemy! The mind boggles. The situation would have strained even a Kafka's imagination.

Be that as it may, I am convinced these Communist "friendly enemies" still maintained certain relations. Among others let me cite:

—transportation of matériel from the People's Republic of China to the Khmer Rouge along the Ho Chi Minh trail. The Khmer Rouge have told me that the Vietnamese shamelessly "borrowed" things from these shipments. But I think at least part of China's gifts must have reached the Cambodians.

—artillery support (especially heavy artillery) that the Vietnamese visibly contributed to important Khmer Rouge operations.

—the many trips regime officials—Khieu Samphan, Ieng Sary, and Co.—took to China and back along the Ho Chi Minh trail . . . at North Vietnamese expense.

The Khmer Rouge have condemned the "criminal egoism" of the North Vietnamese in signing the 1973 agreement with the U.S. that put a stop to the Vietnamese-American war, at least for a time. The halt in the fighting meant all U.S. air and naval forces in the Far East and the Pacific were suddenly disengaged. Their massive strength was then deployed against the Khmer Rouge.

In March, 1973, during my stay in Kampuchea's liberated zone, I witnessed the widespread and merciless bombing and strafing, twenty-four hours a day, of our cities, towns, and villages, our communications network; our archeological treasures (ancient ruins near Kompong Thom), our fields, rice paddies, rubber plantations, even our virgin forests—in short everywhere the Khmer Rouge might take refuge. These extremely deadly American operations never let up, even on Sunday. My wife Monique and I had the honor of experiencing the attacks in the company of Khmer Rouge leaders (including Pol Pot). The bombings and strafings were conducted by the U.S. Air Force from its bases in Thailand. They were incredibly violent and profuse, but fortunately not particularly effective.

Khieu Samphan, Son Sen, and associates, whom I was permitted to see and speak with when I returned to Kampuchea after the victory of April, 1975, impressed me with the bitterness and even hatred they bore toward Hanoi's leaders after the "Vietnamese betrayal" of 1973. They eventually admitted to me that the Vietnamese sellout had allowed them to take Draconian measures aimed at eliminating North Vietnamese and Vietcong presence in Cambodia once and for all.

Earlier the Vietnamese had made themselves completely at home in Kampuchea. They got a degree of cooperation from Kampucheans in the military, political, ideological, economic, social domains. After I left the liberated zone (April, 1973) and returned to Peking, the Khmer

Rouge decided to make the Viets feel much less at home. They arbitrarily regrouped the Vietnamese population of each *khum* (commune), each *srok* (district) into cooperatives that quickly turned into virtual concentration camps, since their inhabitants had no choice but to live there and no means of communicating in any way with the Vietnamese and their bases.

That is how, starting in 1973, the Khmer Rouge emptied our Tonlé Sap (Great Lake), our lakes, and our rivers of their Vietnamese inhabitants (the Vietnamese were primarily fishermen). In 1969 there were more than 400,000 ethnic Vietnamese in Kampuchea. After their coup, Lon Nol and his supporters eliminated or banished to South Vietnam at least half of these Yuons. The Khmer Rouge finished the job between 1973 and 1975, as I had it from Khieu Samphan. In 1979 Radio Hanoi confirmed the Pol Pot regime's murder or massive repatriation of Kampuchea's Vietnamese residents.

Beyond any doubt, Pol Pot displayed a profound fascination with Hitler in his speeches and press conferences. Disturbingly, the name came up again and again: "We are no Hitlers! Only Hitler was capable of genocide!" "Hitler, Hitler, Hitler . . ." Pol Pot obviously enjoyed his obsessive name-dropping. His genocide of Vietnamese men, women, and children, like Lon Nol's, bore a strange resemblance to Hitler's holocaust . . .

Shortly after the Americans and Vietnamese signed their cease-fire agreement in Paris in 1973, the Khmer Rouge requested, with deliberate abruptness, that the Vietnamese dismantle their military and other bases in Kampuchea and purely and simply clear out of Cambodian territory. The Vietnamese never complied with the Khmer Rouge leaders' order to evacuate. Quite to the contrary, they strengthened their system of military occupation of Kampuchea and continuously upgraded their spy network and their subversive activities, going so far as to "vietminhize" a growing number of Khmer Rouge (Pol Pot supporters), especially in the military zone known as 203, which includes a part of Kompong Cham province (the districts of Krek and Memot), part of Prey Veng province (district of Kamchay Mea), part of Kratié province (Snuol district) and part of Svay Rieng province (the famous "Parrot's Beak").

The Vietnamese efforts to "depolpotize" their Khmer Rouge comrades constituted a kind of revenge. So Pol Pot liquidated the Khmer Vietminh? Never mind that, they said to themselves, we'll just "khmervietminhize" the Khmer Rouge! This is what might be called Vietnamese perseverance. And it is what Ieng Sary, deputy Prime Minister in charge of foreign affairs, told his diplomat friends were "Vietnamese attempts at a coup d'état to overthrow Democratic Kampuchea"!

The coup in question would not succeed until January 7, 1979, with a blitzkrieg by Vo Nguyen Giap's *wehrmacht*. The object was to replace Pol Pot, Ieng Sary, and Khieu Samphan with Heng Samrin, Chea Sim, and Ros Samay. The new leaders had not been Khmer Vietminh during the war of 1970–1975, but rather Pol Pot supporters. In fact the purges Pol Pot and Ieng Sary ordered from 1976 on, aimed at a growing splinter group within their own party, unwittingly helped the Vietnamese turn a good number of Khmer Vietminh into Khmer Rouge—including Heng Samrin, Chea Sim, and Ros Samay!

But let us now return to the question my readers will most certainly ask me: "You tell us the Vietnamese and the Khmer Rouge were constantly arguing, tearing each other to pieces, killing each other off. Then how did they finally win out over Lon Nol, the Americans, and their Saigon allies?"

The question is highly logical *a priori*. The appropriate answer is this: today it is commonly held that Pol Pot and his followers are 100 percent pro-Chinese and just as anti-Vietnamese. But it should be kept in mind that China loyally helped Vietnam until the end of the anti-American war in Indochina. China enabled Vietnam to overcome its terrible financial and economic difficulties on the one hand, and on the other to fight to the finish against the Americans. Even after President Richard Nixon's "surprise" state visit to the People's Republic of China and the resounding Shanghai communiqué it resulted in—jointly signed by China's Prime Minister (Zhou Enlai) and the American chief executive, China never "dropped" Vietnam, especially as concerns military, material, financial, economic, and medical aid. They were granted on the same large scale as Russian aid to the Democratic Republic of Vietnam.

With that in mind, it is not difficult imagine why the Khmer Rouge had to cooperate with the Vietnamese in Kampuchea, willingly or not, essentially on the military and operational levels. Nor should it be forgotten that in April, 1970, the People's Republic of China enthusiastically hosted the "Summit Conference of Indochinese Peoples." The object of the conference was to seal the political, economic, and above all military pact binding the four Indochinese Communist entities: FUNK Kampuchea, the Democratic Republic of Vietnam, the Republic of South Vietnam (Vietcong), and the Pathet Lao. It was an official alliance and the Khmer Rouge subscribed to it. Within this formal framework, the Democratic Republic of Vietnam committed itself to keeping the Ho Chi Minh trail supply routes open for the Khmer Rouge despite intensive bombing and shelling by American airpower. Furthermore, North Vietnamese armed forces were at the front trying to contain the redoubtable American invasion (more than 50,-000 infantrymen and hundreds of armored units, supported by strong artillery and very diversified airpower) as well as Saigon President Nguyen Van Thieu's well-equipped armed forces (more than 100,000 men).

The indisputably effective and heroic shield the North Vietnamese provided during these first months of war (starting in March–April, 1970) allowed the fledgling Khmer Rouge armed forces to develop and grow stronger, so that five years later, in April, 1975, they were able to drive the Americans out of Cambodia and take possession of Phnom Penh and the country's other large towns.

Pol Pot and his men, of course, have imperturbably stated for all to hear that the tiny Khmer Rouge army single-handedly stood up to the formidable American and South Vietnamese invaders. In all seriousness Pol Pot, Ieng Sary, Khieu Samphan, Son Sen, Nuon Chea (President of the Popular Assembly) asserted over the radio (first from the *maquis*, then in Phnom Penh) that with rudimentary and primitive weapons their troops succeeded in wiping out almost all of the enemy infantry divisions, armored divisions, and airpower.

There is nothing wrong with being patriotic, but deliberately adopting a chauvinistic and dishonest attitude, to the point of denying that the North Vietnamese allies and comrades-at-arms played a preponderant role, to say the least, in stopping, then pushing back the American and South Vietnamese invaders in 1970, 1971, and 1972, is not only insulting to those allies but also an insult to history.

Time will inevitably uncover dishonesty and lies; history has no room for them. And it does not reflect badly on one's own people to behave gallantly, or at least to observe fair play, toward a comrade-at-arms, the more so when facing a common adversary or enemy.

Far be it from me to conceal the sometimes sublime heroism of my Khmer Rouge compatriots (in their capacity as fighters). But it is unseemly for Kampuchean patriots to make themselves look ridiculous to the whole world with the bald-faced assertion that "with kitchen knives, bows and arrows, and a few old rifles, we were able from the start to destroy hundreds of American cannons, airplanes, fighter-helicopters, tanks." Distorting the facts in this way means stripping the heroic Khmer Rouge *yotheas*' real exploits of their credibility.

Let us render unto Caesar that which is Caesar's. Let us frankly admit that in the so-called Khmer Rouge victories of 1971, 1972, and 1973 over American, South Vietnamese, and Lon Nol forces, at the Cambodia-Vietnam border as well as within the country—the battles of Kirirom, Pich Nil (Route 4), Kompong Som, Kampot, Route 5 (Kompong Chhnang), Kompong Cham, Kompong Thom (Chenla I, Chenla II)—Vietnamese artillery and tanks, as well as their numerous infantry divisions, made a very important contribution, not to say a decisive one. For until the end of the war (April, 1975), the Khmer Rouge army never came up with any real armored units or artillery. They had nothing but infantry units. Their "artillery" consisted essentially of light cannon—and rocket-launchers! As for what (small) rockets they had, there were no launching pads for them. The Khmer Rouge improvised some out of bamboo for their 1973–1975 bombing of Phnom Penh, and they did not hit one of their military objectives. Instead, residential neighborhoods of no military interest were bombed, markets and schools were destroyed, children and innocent adults were killed or hideously wounded —all for nothing. The sensational destruction of a part of the Pochentong airbase (in 1970), the gas tanks at Kilometer 6, the oil refinery at Kompong Som (formerly Sihanoukville), the strategic bridge over the Tonle Sap, were the work of Vietnamese engineer corpsmen or suicide commandos, with Cambodian "patriots" as their guides.

Hanoi, naturally enough, displayed and continues to display remarkable modesty and discretion regarding exploits of this nature in Kampuchea. They always gave credit for them to the FUNK armed forces. Today we know the Socialist Republic of Vietnam has officially and historically attributed even the blitzkrieg of late December, 1978 to early January, 1979 to the insignificant army of Heng Samrin, Hanoi's number-one puppet!

Now that we have taken care of Caesar, let us examine the case of the Khmer Rouge fighters, both men and women. First of all, there can be no doubt that Pol Pot and Son Sen were able to levy a strong army, one of truly uncommon courage, after several years of persistent indoctrination and harsh training. There are three reasons for this exceptional success:

• *The method of recruitment:* Poor peasants, mountain people, the inhabitants of forest regions and the most remote villages, those most "neglected" by the old regime, were exclusively recruited. To what end? Clever propaganda filled their hearts and minds with a seething, unquenchable hatred for the "upper classes": those who were well housed, clothed, and fed; who could send their children to school, not needing them at home to help in the fields or tend the cattle or buffalo; who owned real and personal property, had servants, etc.; who could easily pay their taxes, or who collected them; those who administered or governed—in a word, the "oppressors."

• *The use of children:* Once they were enlisted in the revolutionary army, these children were separated from their families, removed from their home villages to Pol Pot's indoctrination camps. They began their military careers at the age of twelve. Taken in hand so young, these *yothea*s were convinced before long that the party was doing them the greatest of honors by naming them *oppakar phdach kar robas pak,* literally, "the dictatorial instrument of the party."

Being the dictatorial instrument of the party meant having the command of "troops of workers"—those who were not members of the party, those (including intellectuals and ex-students) who had been marched out of the towns and rich villages following the end of the war (in April, 1975), and those who had been members of the FUNK (including former ambassadors of the GRUNK) whom the party had not yet decided to liquidate. Being the dictatorial instrument of the party also meant having the power of life or death over all categories of slaves. It meant having the right to any food available in cooperatives or in the wild (fruit, meat, etc.), while the common herd of civilians received only a daily ration strictly meted out by the local "President," a Pol Pot–Ieng Sary minion. In addition it meant being able to forage in the cities, with their abandoned grocery stores, shops, garages; a chance to play the city dweller. And then it was lots of fun to play soldiers for real, with real, really deadly weapons. During the final years of their reign, Lon Nol's generals had used a similar strategem to attract cannon fodder: they mobilized twelve-year-olds with the tantalizing prospect of playing war, using guns that were pretty—and better yet, really worked. Unlike Lon Nol's recruits, however, the young Khmer Rouge soldiers were often motivated by true patriotic feeling, backed up by solid ideological indoctrination. The Khmer Rouge child-soldiers had no reason to hate Pol Pot's inhuman regime. They had never known and so could not remember what life was like under Sihanouk. They sincerely believed what they were told about the "old society": that it was despicable, contemptible, corrupt, unjust, oppressive in the extreme.

• *The School for Cruelty:* "Habit in youth becomes nature in age," the saying goes. A wine-loving Frenchman in America might sometimes resign himself to drinking a glass of milk or Coca-Cola with a meal, but if his host gives him a choice of drinks he will invariably ask for a glass of wine, not even caring if it comes from California. Likewise, Pol Pot and Ieng Sary quite rightly thought that if they trained their young recruits on cruel games, they would end up as soldiers with a love of killing and consequently of war.

During the three years I spent with the Khmer Rouge under house arrest in Phnom Penh, I saw the *yothea*s in charge of guarding my "camp" constantly take pleasure in tormenting animals (dogs, cats, monkeys, geckos). At the same time, they often complained about not being sent to the front where they could "knock off some Viets." The most wonderful thing Pol Pot and Ieng Sary could do for their soldiers was simply send them to the front line to meet the enemy. Khmer Rouge fighters, both men and women, were then and are now perfectly oblivious of the fear of death or injury. On that score, they must be given credit. The Khmer Rouge loved to make their victims suffer as much as possible, but they also overcame their own physical suffering with astonishing ease and remained perfectly stoical in the worst of personal circumstances. My wife Monique and I were able to observe a few of these "super soldiers" in the former Khmer-Soviet Friendship Hospital (renamed the April 17, 1975, Hospital) and in certain provinces. With that kind of men and women in their ranks, the Khmer Rouge were able to drive the Americans out of Phnom Penh, slaughter the pathetic Lon Nol troops, and simultaneously excel at "knocking off Viets."

·

WHY DID THE U.S. LOSE
THE WAR IN CAMBODIA?

The question of America's misadventures in Cambodia does not figure *a priori* in this book; our specific study is the Khmer Rouge–Vietnamese conflict.

However, I consider this the opportune moment to satisfy my readers' curiosity on that count.

At this juncture my readers could legitimately hypothesize that the heroism of the Vietnamese fighters and Khmer *yothea*s does not suffice to explain the defeat of the world's most powerful nation, the more so since as Khieu Samphan told me in 1978 while he was head of the Khmer Rouge state, "our soldiers beat the Americans, but during the war against the U.S. and Lon Nol, our number-one enemy was really the Vietnamese."

Since heroic fighting alone does not account for the Khmer-Vietnamese defeat of the U.S. and its allies, the following factors should also be considered:

• *The underestimation by Nixon, Lon Nol, and Sirik Matak of Sihanouk.* Their anti-Sihanouk coup of March, 1970, was motivated by the ironclad belief that Norodom Sihanouk had become extremely unpopular with his countrymen, including the peasants, his most faithful partisans, who finally turned against him. The best-known example is the revolt in Samlaut, Battambang province. It was in fact a peasant uprising against Lon Nol's army; the Khmer Rouge made full political use of the army's extortion in the provinces. Furthermore, the above-named trio believed no less firmly that Sihanouk, "discouraged, disillusioned, despairing," would not be able to meet the challenge and lead a resistance movement. Finally, they cal-

culated that even if Sihanouk dared proclaim his resistance, his movement would not be supported by the Khmer
Rouge, the prince's deadly enemies, nor by the USSR, nor
by the People's Republic of China. Yet all of these optimis-
tic certainties (except concerning the Soviets' attitude)
were belied by subsequent events: Norodom Sihanouk's
appeals of March 19 and 23, 1970, were heard and supported by a large portion of the Khmer population and the
Khmer Rouge themselves, and strongly backed by the People's Republic of China, the Democratic People's Republic
of Korea, the Federal Socialist Republic of Yugoslavia
(Marshal Tito), the Socialist Republic of Romania (President Ceausescu), the People's Socialist Republic of Albania
(President Enver Hoxha), the Republic of Cuba (President
Castro), Algeria (President Boumédienne), and most of the
Arab and African nations, not to mention the Democratic
Republic of Vietnam and the Vietcong. The massacre by
Lon Nol's army (on the outskirts of Phnom Penh, in Takeo,
Prey Veng) of Khmer patriots and peasants who had re-
sponded to Sihanouk's appeal, prompted an impressive
number of citizens to join the *maquis* and caused an ir-
remediable split in Khmer unity, to the great detriment of
the U.S.–Lon Nol faction.

• *Underestimation of the Khmer Rouge's political
sense.* Lon Nol, Sirik Matak, and their clique, trusting their
own superior intelligence, thought the Khmer Rouge
would easily be lured by their two-part invitation: to join
them as anti-Sihanouk republicans, and to take part in a
government of "reconciliation and national unity." The
Khmer Rouge, however, while they did not become Sihanouk supporters, opted to side with Sihanouk instead of
Lon Nol. They planned to get rid of the Prince and his
followers after the projected Communist victory.

• *Underestimation of the Viets:* In the minds of the Pentagon experts and of Nixon, Lon Nol, and Sirik Matak, the American and South Vietnamese military invasion of May to July, 1970, would make a clean sweep of Viet sanctuaries in Cambodia and irreversibly drive out their occupants. Then their war effort would no longer be handicapped by the sanctuaries, which were like so many knives in their backs. At the same time, the United States would add another satellite state to Thailand: the Khmer Republic, a new base for American aggression against Vietnam. On this subject, President Richard Nixon went so far as to state for all to hear that the annexation of Cambodia was the "best investment" he had ever made for the United States during his "long political career." Later events have disproved all these calculations by the tactical wizards of Washington, Saigon, and Phnom Penh. During the royal government period, the Viet sanctuaries were minuscule and limited to a few outlying and uninhabited sectors along the Cambodia–Vietnam borderline. They visibly expanded and swelled in size shortly after Lon Nol's coup d'état; then they spread through the whole of the self-proclaimed Khmer Republic. The large-scale invasion of Kampuchea by 200,000 American and Saigonese infantrymen, tank crews, and aviators (April, 1970) ended (July, 1970) in a disgraceful fiasco due to the strength of the brand-new military alliance of the North Vietnamese, the Sihanouk supporters, and the Khmer Rouge. This alliance had been made official in Canton in April, 1970, with the blessing of Prime Minister Zhou Enlai, the enthusiastic host of the Summit Conference of Indochinese Peoples.

• *Corruption in the Lon Nol–Sirik Matak government* was such that the regime's officers and soldiers did not hesitate to sell arms, munitions, medicine, surgical supplies, etc., to the North Vietnamese and the Khmer Rouge, whom China (and also the Democratic Republic of Korea, to a lesser extent) provided each year with an appreciable quantity of American dollars and other strong currencies. Moreover, it was common knowledge that both the U.S. and Lon Nol's military staffs in Kampuchea were riddled with Vietnamese and Khmer Rouge spies.

• *The permission the "Khmer Republic" regime gave the armed forces of Nguyen Van Thieu's pro-American (Saigon) regime to occupy Cambodian territory indefinitely, to pillage,* kill, and rape ended up alienating all young people, all intellectuals, and all citizens taking pride in their nation, from Lon Nol and his regime.

• *The "Khmer Republic" leaders proved incapable of maintaining or safeguarding national independence and territorial integrity;* but what is more, they progressively let themselves be dominated by the American imperialists and even by Thieu's South Vietnamese and to a certain extent by the Thais. This obvious and ignominious loss of national sovereignty and dignity alienated a very great number of the government's initial supporters. It tipped the scales in favor of the FUNK, meaning the Khmer Rouge.

• *Intensive U.S. Air Force bombing of "Resistance Kampuchea" was manifestly ineffectual.* This is, incidentally, how my wife Monique and I were easily able to survive in the liberated zone in March, 1973, despite the impressive and persistent closeness of diversified bombing and strafing attacks, day in and day out.

• *To the very end (April 17, 1975), the Khmer Rouge were wily enough to convince everyone*—Buddhist monks, city dwellers, rural refugees in the as-yet-"unliberated" cities, and even Lon Nol's soldiers—that if they wanted Samdech Norodom Sihanouk back in power (which is what almost everyone wanted after 1971!) they should help the FUNK (meaning the Khmer Rouge) oust the U.S.–Lon Nol faction as quickly as possible.

At dawn on April 17, 1975, the day of the "great Khmer Rouge victory," a good number of Lon Nol units around Phnom Penh and in the capital itself enthusiastically laid down their arms without waiting for the Khmer Rouge troops to arrive or even come into view. They believed the Khmer Rouge's "whisper campaign" to the effect that Samdech Euv would leave Peking immediately —by plane—once Phnom Penh fell to the Khmer Rouge, and land at Pochentong. Battambang and certain other cities followed the same scenario (April 17 and 18, 1975): a good number of Lon Nol units were happy to lay down their arms in the absolute certainty that Samdech Euv would return immediately once the Khmer Rouge took their respective cities.

What happened next was horrible, according to Cambodian refugees who witnessed it. The Sihanouk-supporting Lon Nol troops were savagely slaughtered by the Khmer Rouge. Sihanouk himself had to wait several months in Peking and Pyongyang before the Khmer Rouge would let him come and see his unfortunate country and its people, the victims of the new rulers of Kampuchea and their holocaust.

• *Finally, the historic Watergate scandal in Washington* had a part to play. The hawkish Richard Nixon was replaced by the indecisive, less warlike Gerald Ford. Liberal and pacifist American legislators (Mike Mansfield, Edward Kennedy, George McGovern, etc.), moreover, were in favor of American withdrawal from Kampuchea and with-drawal of support from the Lon Nol–Sirik Matak–Long Boret regime in Phnom Penh. All these factors tipped the scales very heavily in favor of the FUNK and GRUNK—meaning, in the final analysis, the Khmer Rouge.

7

APRIL 17, 1975: THE GREATEST DATE IN THE KAMPUCHEA'S HISTORY, WHICH QUICKLY TURNED INTO A NEW NATIONAL CATASTROPHE

It was no exaggeration for the Khmer Rouge to say that their April 17, 1975, victory over American imperialism and its Saigon and Phnom Penh lackeys was the most glorious in Kampuchea's two-thousand-year history. From the sixth to the twelfth centuries our Khmer people and its sovereigns won great victories over many enemies from countries near and far, but the defeat of American imperialism is a unique exploit in the Cambodia's annals of war, rich as they are in wondrous victories.

Unfortunately, victory went to Pol Pot's head. He began comparing himself to history's greatest conquerors (Alexander the Great, Julius Caesar, Napoleon, Hitler). This was apparent to anyone listening closely to his speeches and press conferences in 1977 and 1978, and to the unsettling propaganda broadcast every day over Radio Phnom Penh by the Kampuchean Communist Party (meaning Pol Pot himself) from 1975 until January 7, 1979, when Vo Nguyen Giap's blitzkrieg brought down Phnom Penh. Never in the human memory has a leader (be he an emperor or dictator), a government, or a political party in power sung its own praises in such a dithyrambic, insolent, deceitful, shameless, and immodest way as the Pol Pot–Ieng Sary regime did. As Radio Hanoi has since stated, Messrs. Pol Pot and Ieng Sary outstripped even their guru, the late Joseph Goebbels, when it came to propaganda!

In September, 1975, the first time I returned to "liberated" Cambodia at the invitation of the Khmer Rouge leaders, I was most surprised to hear Khieu Samphan, Son Sen, and Co. tell me, all smiles and looking perfectly pleased, that their soldiers were "unhappy" with the Party because it would not give them the green light to recapture "Kampuchea Krom"—that is, lower Cambodia (South Vietnam)—as well as the border districts along the Thai frontier that had once belonged to Cambodia (Aranya, Surin, etc.).

Son Sen, Vice Prime Minister in Charge of National Defense, claimed his glorious "revolutionary army of Kampuchea" felt it could make quick work of General Giap's army, not to mention Kukrit Pramoj and Kriangsak Chamanond's much less imposing Thai army.

But between the months of April and September, 1975, there had already been several encounters (on both land and sea) between Communist Vietnam and Communist Cambodia, not to mention a few Khmer Rouge incursions into the skittish Thais' territory. The most serious of the Cambodian-Vietnamese encounters was in June and July, 1975. At stake was the Wai Island group, a likely base for possible offshore oil-drilling operations. The islands had always been governed by Cambodia. However, during the 1950s, Saigon's U.S.-backed dictator, Ngo Dinh Diem, made an official claim to Wai and a number of Cambodia's other coastal islands. Norodom Sihanouk categorically rejected these insane demands, and Ngo Dihn Diem desisted.

Then came Lon Nol's coup d'état, overthrowing Norodom Sihanouk. Diem's successor in Saigon, Nguyen Van Thieu, took advantage of the situation to annex most of Cambodia's coastal islands. Lon Nol and Sirik Matak did not protest, since they needed the help of Thieu's armed forces in Kampuchea to keep them in power in Phnom Penh.

In late April, 1975, the Cambodian and Vietnamese

Communists, giddy with victory, wasted no time in claiming the Wai group and another secondary (Cambodian) island by force. They also demanded a "favorable delineation" of the Cambodian-Vietnamese border, despite the fact it is well established and clearly marked on maps made during the French Colonial period as well as on more recent American-made maps.

Shortly after the March 18, 1970, coup d'état in Phnom Penh, North Vietnam's Prime Minister Pham Van Dong called on me in Peking, and in the presence of China's Prime Minister Zhou Enlai, swore to me in the name of his country that the Democratic Republic of Vietnam would always respect the abovementioned delineation of territorial borders, as well as the "Kingdom of Cambodia's" coastal islands.

In the euphoria surrounding the close of the Summit Conference of Indochinese Peoples (April, 1970), Pham Van Dong promised Norodom Sihanouk, again in Zhou Enlai's presence, that after our "joint victory over American imperialism," he and I would together go and lay a monumental "friendship marker" somewhere along the Vietnam-Cambodia border. It would symbolize the two countries' mutual respect of each other's territorial integrity and national independence. The Khmer Rouge have never forgiven Communist Vietnam for violating these promises made to Cambodia . . . via Norodom Sihanouk!

Now that we have analyzed these irrefutable border violations, I would like to call my readers' attention to a certain number of disturbing facts:

—In 1978 President Khieu Samphan confided in me that his soldiers (Khmer Rouge) were "unstoppable" as far as the Kampuchea-Vietnamese war went: every time they saw sugar palms (*thnots,* in the Khmer language) in Kampuchea Krom territory (South Vietnam), these patriot-soldiers could not help crossing the border and advancing, irresistibly drawn toward the Khmer *thnots.*

—A few years earlier, in August, 1975, while I was in Pyongyang as the guest of President Kim Il Sung of the Democratic People's Republic of Korea, the North Vietnamese chargé d'affaires there told me (in the course of an audience I had granted him at my residence on Lake Chang Su On) that taking into account my protests against the Wai Islands' occupation by the Democratic Republic of Vietnam's naval and armed forces, his country would agree to evacuate the islands in question and "provisionally entrust the Phnom Penh government with their administration." I asked the chargé d'affaires for assurances that Vietnam recognized Way Island as being Cambodian territory. He refused to answer my request. In 1978, Radio Hanoi proclaimed that the island group out-and-out "belonged to the Socialist Republic of Vietnam"!

—During the same audience, the same Vietnamese diplomat told me that the Vietnam-Cambodia conflict had been started by Kampuchea as an undeclared war. According to this version, Kampuchea "unleashed several thousand *yotheas* against Vietnam" shortly after the victory of April, 1975. The object was "to occupy a large portion of South Vietnam along the Cambodian border and work toward exterminating the Vietnamese population." He then acquainted me with the details of Khmer Rouge atrocities in Vietnam. They were identical to those later reported in Thai border villages. Furthermore, they validate information Cambodian refugees from Pol Pot's living hell have provided concerning the Khmer Rouge's behavior toward their own compatriots within their own country.

Who is really to blame for the war of 1975, Communist

Cambodia or North Vietnam? The responsibility is no doubt shared, as we shall see in the following chapters. Specifically, it will be established that the Pol Pot–Ieng Sary regime did everything possible to plunge Kampuchea and its unfortunate people into a new national catastrophe. But the Socialist Republic of Vietnam's conduct was just as reprehensible. There can be no doubt of its land-hungry and hegemonic intentions toward Cambodia. As proof I only need cite the 1978 radio broadcast stating that the Wai group was Vietnamese and the all too obvious protectorate status of Heng Samrin's Kampuchea since January 7, 1979.

8

THE LON NOL AND POL POT FACTIONS MADE THE SAME FATAL MISTAKES CONCERNING THE VIETNAMESE

Taking their version of history as their witness, the Lon Nol–Sirik Matak camp sentenced me to death in 1970 for "high treason to the benefit of the Vietnamese Communists." Shortly after the victory of April 17, 1975, the Pol Pot government began daily radio broadcasts condemning the Khmer monarchy for "selling out to the Vietnamese" and having "ceded" Kampuchea Krom to them.

In March, 1970, the Lon Nol–Sirik Matak government declared it would proceed to rid Kampuchea of "ignoble" Vietnamese presence. It went right to work—with cowardly murders of Vietnamese residents, the seizure of their real and personal property. A favorite job was raping Vietnamese women deemed "worth the trouble."

A few days after this memorable pogrom or genocide in best Hitlerian style, the so-called Khmer Republicans were reduced to having to make an official appeal to Saigon, meaning that Nguyen Van Thieu's savage horde came to invade, pillage, burn, ruin, destroy Cambodia, and to rob, torture, rape, and murder Cambodians. That was the high price Nguyen Van Thieu's government made Cambodia pay in exchange for the military protection it provided the faltering Khmer Republic. Also included were other terrible and humiliating concessions the leaders (after a fashion) in Phnom Penh would later have to make:

—Saigon troops evacuated many Khmer villages along the Vietnamese border. The homeless inhabitants then took refuge in the cities, most notably Svay Rieng and

Phnom Penh. Their living conditions were pitiful. Thieu then "gave" the deserted villages—houses, livestock, fowl, fruit trees, fields, rice paddies, and all—to Vietnamese families victimized by Lon Nol and Sirik Matak in March–April, 1970. Moreover, Vietnam's literal colonization of these Khmer villages in 1970–1971 led to later run-ins between the Vietnamese (North Vietnamese and Vietcong) and the Khmer Rouge, in May through July, 1975. The Cambodian Communists quite rightly wanted to recover the border villages Vietnam had so brazenly annexed. However, it was obviously wrong of the Khmer Rouge (once they had won back the border villages and, according to Radio Hanoi, savagely slaughtered their Vietnamese inhabitants) to advance deep into Vietnam. This was their way of taking revenge on Nguyen Van Thieu's crimes: sending their troops to annex a part of South Vietnam!

–After April, 1970, Thieu also annexed a large and strategic town on the Mekong, with the Lon Nol–Sirik Matak government's tacit consent. Neak Luong, about fifty kilometers from Phnom Penh, was officially dubbed "Saigon Moi" (New Saigon) by the Vietnamese army. Here, too, Thieu's soldiers drove the original inhabitants out of their homes, villages, fields. They were then forced *manu militari* toward the nearby town of Prey Veng and to Phnom Penh. Again, local villages—houses, fields and all —were "granted" to the Vietnamese men and women who had suffered at the hands of Phnom Penh's new masters.

—The Saigon army further decreed that the Khmer border town of Kompong Trach (Kampot province) was henceforth a "permanent base of the Republic of (South) Vietnam's armed forces."

—President Thieu's navy took possession of nearly all the coastal islands dependent upon Kampot province. Vietnamese fishermen were given carte-blanche fishing rights in Khmer territorial waters off Kampot and Kep, ruining Khmer fishermen—and the Cambodian economy.

—Thieu's army assumed the right to ship all it wanted of the Cambodians' cattle, buffalo, cars, machines, etc., back to South Vietnam. It went so far as to send giant helicopters to scavenge in Khmer territory. Equipped with hooks and steel cables, they lifted cars (private property) and industrial equipment (starting at the rubber plantation in Kompong Cham). Thieu's men also ransacked several Buddhist monasteries, which had housed ancient and price-less cultural treasures.

Convinced of their role as redeemers, Lon Nol and Sirik Matak decided simply to declare war on Vietnam. Lon Nol even talked about a "holy war": heaven had entrusted him with the "holy mission" of driving the "evil genius" embod-ied in the Vietnamese out of Kampuchea. The Lon Nol government's propaganda also asserted that Sihanouk was a "demon" sent by the "king of Hell" to help the *Thmils* (North Vietnamese and Vietcong monsters) destroy Bud-dhism.

Here I must digress for a moment. The Lon Nol faction claimed I had taken millions of dollars from the Viet-namese and the Americans, while the truth was that during the 1960s Lon Nol and those close to him had done some very lucrative business with the Vietnamese (selling rice and pharmaceuticals, shipping arms and ammunition at very high prices, etc.). Today my family and I have nothing left and live on the charity of the People's Republic of China, while Lon Nol's closest associates and Lon Nol him-self live in comfort in luxury in America, France, and other countries.

The outcome of Lon Nol's holy war is common knowl-

edge, already part of history. Thanks to the so-called
Khmer Republic, the Buddhist religion, which had flour-
ished under Sihanouk, was completely eradicated once the
crusading Lon Nol government was defeated by the Communists in April, 1975. The "Republicans" had dared to
challenge the Khmer Rouge to a duel, claiming they would
"pulverize" them within a few months!

Lon Nol . . . Pol Pot: names so similar and in such close
succession that after the Khmer Rouge victory of April 17,
1975, the North Vietnamese were once again challenged by
"tough" Kampuchea. It was a fateful challenge; everyone
is acquainted with the catastrophic results (January, 1979).

But let us begin at the beginning. Pol Pot, like Lon
Nol, was a visionary. According to Khieu Samphan, (his
spokesman, of sorts, to Sihanouk in his "retirement"), it
appeared that the Vietnamese threat with a capital T was
like a malignancy eating away at Kampuchea just as cancer would a human body. Son Sen, Pol Pot's war minister,
had already told me in September, 1975, that to save Kampuchea and the Khmer people from utterly disappearing,
the "Vietnamese sickness would have to be totally eradicated." This "cancer" would require a "three-part surgical
operation."

Following Son Sen's example, Khieu Samphan made a
point of explaining this "three-part operation" to me several times during our (rare) conversations between 1976
and 1978:

1. Categorically refusing Vietnamese citizens, who-
ever they might be, the right to live in Cambodia. The
Khmer Rouge's efforts in this direction were the physical
liquidation of a large number of Vietnamese residents
"suspected of being agents or spies for the Vietminh or

Vietcong" and the forced repatriation of all other Vietnamese residents. This was accomplished by the second half of 1973.

2. Giving all Cambodian men and women the order to work twice, ten times as hard as the Vietnamese people, in order, Khieu Samphan told me, to make Kampuchea much stronger than Vietnam from every point of view (military, economic, ideological). According to the Khmer Rouge leaders, this frantic work they were making their people do would turn Kampuchea into an "impregnable fortress." What actually transpired was that the exhausted and disenchanted Khmer people were no longer in any condition to resist when Hanoi unleashed its army.

3. "Accepting" a large-scale engagement with Vietnam: to what end? The problem of Vietnamese sanctuaries had to be fought out; they must be eliminated. A "more just" delineation of the land and sea borders between Kampuchea and Vietnam was also necessary. Finally, the threat of Soviet-Viet expansionism had to be met head on. Without Democratic Kampuchea to stop it, it would end up spreading through the rest of Southeast Asia and even farther. January 7, 1979, showed just what was to gain from such large-scale armed conflict!

THE "LITTLE MUSSOLINIS" WHO THOUGHT THEY WERE BETTER THAN NAPOLEON OR HITLER

In April, 1970, during the Summit Conference of Indochinese Peoples that I had helped organize, Premier Pham Van Dong of the Democratic Republic of Vietnam said to me: "Your Highness, we earnestly wish to see you resume your functions as Cambodia's head of state as soon as possible. We Vietnamese are your faithful allies; we will fight to the finish for your just cause. But the truth is the Khmers should liberate Phnom Penh on their own. Vietnamese soldiers must not be in evidence. So you will have to wait a few more years until the FAPLNK [Kampuchean People's Armed Forces of National Liberation] can stand on its own as an army. We Vietnamese will help you with all our resources and in all good faith."

In my proclamation of March 23, 1970, I chose the name FAPLNK for the anti-American and anti–Lon Nol army I believed we Cambodian patriots and resistance fighters must immediately create with technical assistance from the North Vietnamese and Vietcong. They were already involved in the Khmer resistance movement.

As we have seen in the preceding chapters, this union of Khmer Rouge, Sihanouk supporters, and Khmer Vietminh was not to be, despite the willingness of the Vietnamese. The Sihanouk-supporting Khmer nationalists, known in Phnom Penh as "Khmer Romdahs" or Liberation Cambodians, were ultimately decimated, liquidated by the Khmer Rouge. The FAPLNK never materialized. By 1974–1975 the Khmer Rouge had the only real army left in Cambodia, officially called the "Revolutionary Army of Kampu-

chea." Credit for the 1975 victory over American imperialism and its Indochinese vassals, then, goes to the Khmer
Rouge.

Cambodia's Communists were nonetheless gravely
mistaken in believing themselves "infinitely superior to the
Yuons," as their oral and written propaganda incessantly
proclaimed. The Khmer Rouge's inflated self-confidence in
every domain has always reminded me of Mussolini. When
I was a high school student in Saigon in the 1930s, it upset
me to watch newsreels of Mussolini posturing as a "Super
Caesar" to crowds of his countrymen. He tried to measure
up to Hitler with his conquest of Ethiopia in 1936, Albania
in 1939. The Second World War led to Signor Benito Mussolini's downfall, ending tragically in his ignominious execution.

Although the Khmer Rouge leaders had read plenty of
books and articles about Mussolini and Hitler, they never
considered that they too might suffer similar reversals. Pol
Pot admits to a Buddhist upbringing, but does not seem to
believe in the law of karma, the ruling principle of human
life as explained by Buddha more than 2,500 years ago.
Man quite evidently lives, grows older, dies. Buddha
teaches that man dies and is reborn. He lives again, grows
old and dies again, then the cycle continues. But life means
suffering. To alleviate his suffering, man must leave his evil
ways behind and pursue goodness. Only through good conduct and good deeds can man progressively lighten the
burden of his karma (the weight of human existence) until
he has no more karma at all and enters once and for all into
the state of nirvana (the state of non-existence). Another
way of putting it would be to say nirvana is the blissful
cessation of the apparently endless cycle of birth (=suffer-
ing), life (=suffering), illness (=suffering), old age (=suff-
ering), death (=suffering), rebirth (=suffering).

The Khmer Rouge reject Buddha's doctrine with scorn bordering on disgust. During a trip through the provinces we made together in 1976, Khieu Samphan told me: "The real Buddha, the only one that counts, is the people" (meaning the Khmer Rouge directorate). "The people can do anything. The people of Democratic Kampuchea will do the impossible; they are invincible. Anyone who tries to meddle with them will be snuffed out." Khieu Samphan also told me "if we are faithful to the people it does not matter what we do to the Buddhist monks."

Thus the Khmer Rouge believed all they had to do to become "invincible" and annihilate the Yuons was to have their way with Buddhist monks, which really meant stamping out Buddhism, a religion of tolerance, pacifism, and respect for what are commonly known as human rights.

The Khmer Rouge radio no less arrogantly broadcast the following "historic" message from Pol Pot and Ieng Sary: "We are the most powerful government of all, because of our total and definitive defeat of American imperialism, the number one military and economic power in the world. For more than twenty years the Yuons [Democratic Republic of Vietnam] did their best to beat the Americans, but to no avail. The only reason Saigon was liberated on April 30, 1975, and Vietnam subsequently reunited, was because we [the Khmer Rouge] had already undercut the U.S. earlier in April, 1975, and literally pushed the Americans into the sea. The Yuons are weak and cowardly. It does no good for the Soviets to give them colossal amounts of military aid. They are absolutely incapable of putting it to any good use. Even though we have much less sophisticated weaponry than the Yuons and our military equipment is no better than rudimentary [this was barely veiled and unfair criticism of the People's Republic of China, the Khmer Rouge's powerful ally], we can overcome any difficulties and all obstacles. Let there be no mistake! The liberation of South Vietnam, the total defeat of American imperialism in Vietnam, the reunification of Vietnam were all made possible by our military prowess in Kampuchea and the fact that we have given so much help to the Yuons for so many years. We gave them lodging, food, did them countless other favors. Without our help, Ho Chi Minh's followers would have been destroyed long ago by the Americans. So then if this slips the Yuons' minds and they repay our kindness with ingratitude—as their ancestors did our ancestors—we will annihilate them. Under the *Moha Troeum Treuv Moha Phlu Svang Moha Aschar* [literal translation: most serious and just, most farseeing, most formidable] leadership of the Communist Party of Kampuchea (meaning Pol Pot and Ieng Sary), our heroic people and revolutionary army have won incomparable victories, achieved success in all domains, won renown and prestige on all five continents. Not only are we the first Kampuchean regime in two thousand years capable of bringing real independence and national sovereignty to Kampuchea; we are also the rampart ready to foil expansionist attempts by the Soviets and Vietnamese, who want to dominate all of Southeast Asia. Our neighbors and the peoples of the entire world deeply admire us because we set the example of *Ekareach Mchas Kar* [translation: an independent, self-reliant country]. We are making an essential contribution to the peaceful preservation of their liberty and stability."

As the exaggeration of their power and self-worth escalated, the Khmer Rouge on every level of the hierarchy, even my 1976–1978 "jailers" began to believe they were supermen, that they could pulverize the combined armies of Vietnam, the USSR, and the East European Soviet bloc!

In a late 1978 press conference, Pol Pot mentioned in all seriousness the "probability" that Czechoslovakian, Hungarian, Bulgarian, and East German troops would be sent to the rescue of the Vietnamese, Soviet, and Cuban regiments Kampuchea had "put to flight." Pol Pot unblinkingly stated that the Vietnamese were too weak to stand up to the Kampuchean Revolutionary Army "all by themselves." That is why, he continued, the Soviets had had to bring in aviators, tank operators, artillerymen, staff officers from Russia . . . and Cuba. Pol Pot further stated, still with a straight face, that despite these formidable Russo-Cuban reinforcements, the Vietnamese army would be soundly defeated by the Khmer Rouge. He imperturbably predicted that the USSR would soon be compelled to send troops from Eastern Europe "Warsaw Pact member countries" to the aid of the discomfited Vietnamese. Speaking in the learned tones of an expert on guerrilla warfare, Pol Pot gave his journalist "friends" a short course (I wish I could have seen their faces): "We Khmer Rouge are ready to welcome these Bulgarians, Czechs, East Germans, just like we did the Yankees in 1970. . . . They will be decimated by our guerrillas and our country's extremely hot climate, the hardship they experience during the rainy season, and so on." Now his imagination was in high gear. Pol Pot laughingly added: "Since they are used to eating European food, drinking wine or beer every day, we won't have a thing to worry about once they find they can't stomach our water, then run out of rations!"

It is always a mistake to stand in awe of one's enemy. But it is equally dangerous to make light of one's enemy. What is more, Messrs. Pol Pot, Ieng Sary, Khieu Samphan, and Son Sen too readily fantasized all sorts of turns the Kampucheo-Vietnamese war might take, for instance the direct intervention of fighters from Moscow, Havana, even

Prague, Sofia, Budapest, East Berlin, who would die like flies in Kampuchea.

This mythomania eventually spread to the young Khmer Rouge *yothea*s. During my house arrest, my jailers liked to tell us about their "recent exploits at the front." In all probability they were excellent and even heroic fighters. But away from the front they began to imagine they were legendary heroes, or rather, like Daudet's Tartarin de Tarascon, they began to believe in their own tall tales. With genuine conviction they claimed to have slaughtered dozens of Viets at a time, and destroyed tanks, airplanes, and so on with their unsophisticated weapons. Some of these young Khmer Rouge had such sweet faces (like suntanned cherubs) that it was hard to believe they really were the savage and bloodthirsty "dictatorial instruments" of Pol Pot and Ieng Sary's party.

The Khmer Rouge's physical courage cannot be doubted. The problem was they fell into the trap of their own monstrous propaganda machine at a critical moment in their history. In the final analysis, Lon Nol and Pol Pot are like extremes that meet. They were both visionaries who believed in their own superhuman, unearthly invincibility. Lon Nol, the super-believer, and Pol Pot, the super-atheist, agreed on at least one point: they thought they were better than Napoleon or Hitler. They thought it was impossible for their anti-Vietnamese campaign to end up like Waterloo or Stalingrad. For years before his coup of March 18, 1970, Lon Nol had dreamed of reclaiming Kampuchea Krom (South Vietnam) . . . But the fact is the Vietnamese (North and South) toppled his regime and wiped out his self-proclaimed Republic.

10
THE VISCERAL HATRED OF THE VIETNAMESE FELT BY KHMERS OF ALL IDEOLOGICAL PERSUASIONS

For the Lon Nol–Sirik Matak camp, along with Son Ngoc Thanh's contingent, 1968 to 1970 were years of feverish and methodical preparation to depose me (I was of course unaware of their plans). They were helped by the CIA and a few other friends from the so-called free world (see *My War With the CIA,* by Norodom Sihanouk as related to Wilfred Burchett).

The Khmer and foreign plotters concluded, after much covert deliberation, that "the best way to overthrow Norodom Sihanouk without having to deal with too much opposition from his supporters would be officially accusing him of betraying Kampuchea to Vietnamese Communists." This is exactly the tactic they used on March 18, 1970, and during the days, months, and years that followed. It was even bandied about that my wife Monique was a full-blooded Vietnamese, adopted in Saigon by my mother-in-law (Mme. Pomme Peang) and her husband, Monsieur Izzi (a Frenchman!). Lon Nol's progaganda further claimed Mme. Pomme Peang was part Vietnamese, while the only foreign blood she has is a hint of Chinese. Another false accusation was that Mme. Pomme Peang and Monique had accepted lavish gifts from the Hanoi government and the Vietcong, then urged me to betray Kampuchea's independence, sovereignty, territorial integrity, and national dignity to the benefit of the Vietnamese, the Khmer's traditional and mortal enemies!

Once the "Khmer Republic" had fallen, Pol Pot and

Ieng Sary's self-styled "Democratic Kampuchea" also centered its propaganda on the Khmer monarchy's supposed sellout to the Yuons. Khmer Rouge commissars never failed to tell the students in their political propaganda courses, including peasants from the cooperatives, the story of the ancient Khmer king who married a Vietnamese woman, who was then alleged to have had the Khmer port of Saigon given to the Annamites (from Vietnam's Annam province). The Khmer name for Saigon, by the way, is Prey Nokor; *prey* means forest, *nokor* home or city.

Khmer Rouge radio propaganda, not unlike Lon Nol's, blamed the monarchy for all of Kampuchea's past troubles. Their visceral hatred of the monarchy extended to the great Angkor kings (Jayavarman I, Duryavarman II, Jayavarman VII, and others), denying them any share of the Angkor civilization's worldwide renown. They were not even given credit for having considerably enlarged the original Kambuja (Kampuchea); during their reigns it included the greater part of present-day Thailand, Vietnam, and Laos. Pol Pot and his followers stubbornly insisted that "feudalism," meaning the Khmer monarchy, had not once in its two-thousand-year history been able to defend Kampuchea's territorial integrity. The people, they said, had established the nation's territory more than two thousand years ago. According to Pol Pot, the Khmer kings and princes were never able to achieve true national independence for Kampuchea. He labeled the independence won by the country in November 1953 (after Norodom Sihanouk's "crusade") a "sham," calling it "semicolonial status." Yet none of this kept Pol Pot and Ieng Sary from demanding (in 1976–1978) that the Hanoi government hold to the oral and written promises made to Norodom Sihanouk in 1966 and 1967, to wit, their absolute and precise acknowledgement of territorial boundaries, including the coastal islands!

History will judge all this. Without being overly presumptuous, I think it is my duty to reiterate a certain number of facts:

1. It was in 1947, during Norodom Sihanouk's reign, that Cambodia recovered all its territory annexed by Thailand at the start of the Second World War (Battambang province, several districts in the provinces of Siem Reap and Angkor, Oddar Meanchey, Kompong Thom, Preah Vihear, Stung Treng, and Pursat, a part of the Great Lake or Tonlé Sap).

2. It was under Norodom Sihanouk's leadership that Cambodia won its Hague trial in 1962. The International Court of Justice in The Hague officially acknowledged that Cambodia had clear legal title to Preah Vihear and its sacred temple, seized by Thailand a few years earlier. The Court consequently ordered the Bangkok government to give Preah Vihear back to the Khmer kingdom; after a few months of tergiversation, Thailand acquiesced.

3. In 1966–1967, Norodom Sihanouk obtained written statements from the governments of North Vietnam and the Republic of South Vietnam (Vietcong) expressing their official recognition and total acceptance of "Kampuchea's present territorial boundaries, including the coastal islands off Kampot and Kep."

An earlier chapter has given my readers the opportunity to judge just how Lon Nol's so-called Khmer Republic traded on Cambodia's territorial integrity, and how General Nguyen Van Thieu's South Vietnamese profited. Then came the Khmer Rouge; they bragged and continue to brag they have been the only ones in two thousand years capable of establishing and maintaining Kampuchea's territorial integrity. But what has the final result of their anti-Vietnam campaign been?

Today Cambodia is no more than a shambles. The

Kampuchean people have been dismembered, crushed by the unbearable weight of an endless war a few foreign powers are keeping alive . . . until the last Kampuchean is dead. Even today the Khmer Rouge's radio broadcasts are still loudly proclaiming that they are winning victory upon victory over the Viets, that they have "reliberated" an impressive number of cities, towns, ancient temples, districts, communes . . . The fact is, however, that Kampuchea's territorial integrity is shattered. Our country has lost its territorial unity, even its national identity. It has lost its independence, sovereignty, the fabled "national dignity" Pol Pot, Ieng Sary, and Khieu Samphan claimed they had bestowed on Kampuchea for the first time in its two-thousand-year history. And all this has happened because Kampuchea's leaders of the 1970s disdained and steered clear of Norodom Sihanouk's policy of the 1960s, namely the attempt to exorcise our traditional hatred of the Yuons . . . and realistically confront the inevitability of an honorable understanding and fraternal cooperation between two countries which were in the beginning and always shall be placed side by side: as such they must coexist.

11 LOVE YOUR COUNTRY, HELP IT DIE

Because they believed seeking détente with Vietnam meant betraying Cambodia, the Republicans and Communists unanimously charged Norodom Sihanouk with not loving his country.

Now, it may be possible to love a woman passionately and then strangle her like an Othello, or involve her in gunplay like a Prince Rudolf of Austria; even so, the crime must have a motive. But a country cannot be compared to a Desdemona or a Marie Vetsera, dying by the hand of a distraught lover.

Lon Nol and Pol Pot will be able to tell their grandchildren that they killed "their Kampuchea" to save it from Vietnamese domination. Unfortunately it is all too clear that their own anti-Vietnamese mania triggered the Vietnamese threat. I am a chauvinistic enough nationalist to have risked humiliation in order to seek Vietnam's friendship and respect. As far as I am concerned, loving one's country means doing everything in one's power to ensure its survival, independence, honor. There are enough examples in world history to persuade me that a country should never adopt an overambitious policy, especially a foreign policy, and the more so when its means are limited.

I have been criticized for giving various kinds of help to the North Vietnamese and Vietcong in their fight against American imperialism. Lon Nol, Sirik Matak, Son Ngoc Thanh, and their followers sentenced me to death for it, claiming that colonization by the Americans was less serious than the Vietnamese threat. As for myself, I never asked Cambodia to choose between two or three different types of colonialism. All I ever wanted for my country was total independence and unquestioned territorial integrity.

As for the Khmer Rouge, however, they flatly condemned the Khmer monarchy, blaming it for the presence of more than 400,000 Vietnamese residents in Kampuchea. They said that without their own policy of genocide and repatriation of the Vietnamese residents, the latter would have numbered in the tens of millions within a few decades. Thus Kampuchea would become completely dependent upon Vietnam, with the native Kampuchean population reduced to the status of an ethnic minority.

Today the result of this resolutely anti-Vietnamese policy is clear: the military defeat of the Khmer Rouge on January 7, 1979, threw Kampuchea open to an influx of Vietnamese settlers. No one can say how long this influx will last, or if indeed it will ever end; the same thing has been going on in Laos for quite a few years now. (Democratic Kampuchea's Ambassador, Thiounn Prasith, said in a speech to the U.N. Security Council that Phnom Penh's population is currently 90 percent Vietnamese.)

I have also been criticized for opening Kampuchea's doors to the Vietnamese during the 1960s, even to the "most dangerous Yuons," meaning the Vietminh or North Vietnamese Communists. But in the Black Book they distributed at the United Nations in September, 1978, the Khmer Rouge laid a firm claim to the honor of having granted all types of aid and assistance—including huge sanctuaries inside Cambodia—to the Vietminh and Vietcong.

According to the Khmer Rouge, who are "nationalist's nationalists," not Cambodia's Royal Government but *their own* Communist Party of Kampuchea was solely responsible for Cambodia's very early (pre-1960) accessibility to

Vietnamese fighters (see the aforementioned Black Book in the U.N. Library).

Doing everything possible to help a neighbor threatened by imperialism was a duty the kingdom of Cambodia could not shirk. It had approved the mutual responsibilities formulated at the Bandung Conference (first Summit Conference of Asian and African Peoples, 1955). The kingdom of Cambodia and Norodom Sihanouk did not waver in their commitment to the Bandung and Belgrade resolutions (Belgrade: first Summit Conference of Nonaligned Nations, 1960). These resolutions recommended solidarity among all peoples struggling against imperialism, colonialism, and neocolonialism.

At the Belgrade Conference the kingdom of Cambodia became the first non-Arab country to give *de jure* recognition to the provisional government of the fledgling Algerian Republic. This it did at the risk of losing large amounts of French foreign aid. Arab nations have never forgotten the favor Cambodia did the Algerian people at a crucial moment in their history. In March, 1970, the overwhelming majority of Arab countries censured Lon Nol's coup d'état and gave *de jure* recognition to the GRUNK.

Like the Lon Nol camp, the Khmer Rouge objected to my trust in the oral promises and written assurances the Democratic Republic of Vietnam and the Vietcong had made to Kampuchea during the 1960s and after Lon Nol's coup as well.

In their view, the Vietnamese had every fault in the book. Personally, I persist in believing the Vietnamese are no better or worse than any other people. The Khmer Rouge and Lon Nol's supporters are fond of saying the Vietnamese are "bigger ingrates than crocodiles." To the Khmers the crocodile is the symbol of ingratitude. The folk story goes that a Khmer peasant saved a baby crocodile from dying. Despite his poverty, the good fellow then went to great trouble to feed the little creature well. Soon it grew big and strong. One day the crocodile, tired of the same sort of food every day, pushed aside his serving of rabbit or monkey and unceremoniously gulped down his benefactor.

I quite obviously am not unaware of the Hanoi (or Ho Chi Minh City, if you will) Communists' serious faults. Between 1947 and 1954 they caused me some major problems, among which I would mention the following: their armed penetration, even at that early date, into Cambodia, and without my permission; an energetic subversion campaign aimed at "my" peasants, workers, Buddhist monks, and so on; attempts at organizing a "Khmer popular uprising" against the monarchy and Norodom Sihanouk, whom they accused of "selling Cambodia out" to French colonialism; the publication and widespread distribution within Cambodia of anti-Sihanouk, anti-monarchist tracts, pamphlets, and (grotesque) caricatures; deadly ambushes of "my" officials and civil servants; the assassination of many Khmer loyalists; their flagrant role in propagating the First Indochinese War in Cambodia; their repeated sabotage of the kingdom's national economy; their refusal to clear out of Cambodia after the November, 1953, definitive withdrawal of the French and French Union armed forces' troops and command; the fact that five thousand Khmers, legally subjects of His Majesty the King of Cambodia, underwent an intense pro-Communist brainwashing in Hanoi; the aid they gave Pol Pot, Ieng Sary, Khieu Samphan, Son Sen, and their Khmer Rouge between 1955 and 1970 (although it was less than overwhelming).

This unsavory list of Ho Chi Minh's faithful's abuse of

Norodom Sihanouk and his royal regime gives my readers some idea of my personal bitterness toward the Vietnamese. Yet my decision to help them during the 1960s was certainly not financially motivated (let me repeat that I have never taken any money from the Vietnamese and that today, as virtual proletarians, my family and I would not be able to survive without the generosity and fraternal hospitality of the People's Republic of China). I give my word that the reason I decided to cooperate with the Vietnamese was to put Communist Vietnam in Kampuchea's debt in such a way that it would never again dare raise a hand, so to speak, against our country and our people, its benefactors. To do otherwise would bring them total dishonor.

No matter how we feel about them, the Vietnamese always have been and always will be Kampuchea's neighbors. France and Germany have had a similar relationship. Today, however, even the most Germanophobic of Frenchmen has to admit that his country should maintain normal relations with its dangerous neighbor ("democratized" or not). De Gaulle, the number-one anti-German resistance fighter during the Second World War, later saw fit to establish genuinely friendly relations with Germany. Today French President Valéry Giscard d'Estaing and German Chancellor Helmut Schmidt continue De Gaulle and Adenauer's historic work. In like manner the United States and Japan, mortal enemies during World War II, thought it wiser to become friends and even allies once the war was over.

As Cambodia's head of state, my objective in dealing with Vietnam was to keep my country safe. We have seen what kind of foul play Ho Chi Minh, Le Duan, Pham Van

Dong, Vo Nguyen Giap, and the like indulged in between 1947 and 1954. To tell the truth, until 1970 the Vietnamese behaved much better toward Lon Nol, Pol Pot, Ieng Sary, Khieu Samphan, Son Sen, and the like. They had less reason to resent the Vietnamese, then, than Norodom Sihanouk did. But with the fate of an entire state, a country, a people, and a nation in his hands, Sihanouk considered he had no right to risk Kampuchea's very chances of survival.

Sihanouk's attitude toward events was the opposite of Pol Pot and Ieng Sary's words and deeds. It was sheer madness to proclaim over Radio Phnom Penh, as they did in 1978, that "eight million" Kampucheans could and should eliminate fifty million Vietnamese. How would they go about it? The Khmer Rouge leaders actually gave their soldiers the order to kill off the Vietnamese at the rate of thirty per Kampuchean soldier. Their objective was the following: "By sacrificing only two million Kampucheans we (the Khmer Rouge) will be able to eliminate as many as sixty million Vietnamese men and women—and we will still have six million Khmer men and women left to defend our Democratic Kampuchea!"

What about the Vietminh sanctuaries, and the Ho Chi Minh trail crossing a part of Kampuchea? I discussed this with Pham Van Dong when we met in Peking and Canton in March and April, 1970. I told him that after our foreseeable joint victory over the American imperialists and their lackeys, the GRUNK (my royal government) would amicably but firmly request that Pham's Vietnamese unconditionally withdraw.

Visiting Hanoi during the war of 1970–1975, I repeatedly drew the Vietnamese leaders' attention to an article of the Kingdom of Cambodia's constitution stating that in peacetime my country could not allow foreign military installations or troops within its boundaries. Another article of the same law, however, did provide for soliciting armed intervention by nations friendly to Kampuchea's cause, but only if the Khmer kingdom were under attack from one or more hostile foreign powers.

I was adamant, though, on the point that, barring exceptional circumstances, neither Vietnam, the People's Republic of China (our best friend), nor any other power would be allowed to have bases or sanctuaries of any type, including military supply routes, through our country. So Pham Van Dong, Vo Nguyen Giap, and the like promised that "their" Vietnam would "gladly" see to it that their bases, sanctuaries, and soldiers would eventually be removed from Kampuchea for good.

If Cambodia had remained a kingdom—since all the solemn pledges the Vietnamese made were to the Kingdom of Cambodia—or if at the very least Norodom Sihanouk had remained Kampuchea's head of state, would Hanoi really have kept all its promises?

For a clearer understanding of the situation it is indispensable to take a look at each Khmer regime's record with the Vietnamese.

THE LON NOL REGIME

—As early as March, 1970, there were violent anti-Vietnamese demonstrations in Khmer towns and provinces with any appreciable number of Vietnamese residents.

—From the time he was named Prime Minister of the royal government (1969) until his anti-Sihanouk coup d'état on March 18, 1970, Lon Nol seized and redistributed all the arms, ammunition, and military equipment the Chinese,

Russians and other socialist nations sent via Sihanoukville for the North Vietnamese and Vietcong. This he did with Norodom Sihanouk's permission.

—Just before his anti-Sihanouk coup, Lon Nol sent his "Praetorian Guard," disguised as students, into the Phnom Penh embassies of the Democratic Republic of Vietnam and the Republic of South Vietnam (Vietcong), to sack, savagely pillage, and set fire to them.

—With the March 18, 1970, coup, Lon Nol's regime officially rejected the policy of friendship and solidarity with North Vietnam. The self-styled Khmer Republic thus incited Communist Vietnam not to keep the promises it had made to the Kingdom of Cambodia, since that kingdom was obliterated by Lon Nol's men, the country's new masters —acknowledged as such by none other than the United Nations . . . until April 17, 1975!

THE KHMER ROUGE REGIME

The self-styled Democratic Kampuchean government replaced the Khmer Republic on April 17, 1975. What was its policy toward Communist Vietnam, which like Communist Kampuchea had by now emerged victorious from its long struggle with the Americans?

—As early as 1973, the Khmer Rouge massacred tens of thousands of Vietnamese residents accused of being spies or the fifth column of Communist Vietnam. The remaining residents were repatriated to South Vietnam.

—They practiced wide-scale extermination of pro-Vietnam Kampuchean Communists, including Khmer Rouge suspected of being pro-Vietnam.

—Immediately following the signing of the U.S.-Vietnam peace agreement (by Henry Kissinger and Le Duc Tho in Paris, 1973), the Khmer Rouge ordered the Vietminh and Vietcong stationed in Kampuchea out of the country, demanding they dismantle their bases and supply routes. In this way the Khmer Rouge hoped to punish the Viets, "whose government (Hanoi) betrayed the common cause."

—After their victory of April 17, 1975, the Khmer Rouge tried to take over part of Kampuchea Krom (South Vietnam), and in so doing committed horrible atrocities. Many of their victims were Vietnamese civilians (including old people, women, and children). Western journalists, among others, later reported the atrocities they had witnessed in South Vietnam.

—Pol Pot's government rejected all proposals for a peaceful settlement advanced by the Hanoi government (most notably on February 6, 1978).

—Pol Pot's regime stubbornly refused to avail itself of Norodom Sihanouk's services, although even the Chinese considered the prince the only person capable of driving the Vietnamese into a corner, forcing them to respect Kampuchea's sovereignty and its territorial boundaries on land and sea.

—The fact that the Khmer Rouge subjected their own people and even their own followers to genocide, massacres, forced labor, slavery, concentration camps, and political purges horrified the entire world and drove Democratic Kampuchea deeper into isolation each day.

In 1978, Democratic Kampuchea was no longer really supported by the People's Republic of China, the Democratic People's Republic of Korea (Pyongyang), the Socialist Republic of Romania, Japan, and some ASEAN member countries. The regime's unjustifiable stamping out of Buddhism, Islam, Catholicism, and other religions in Kampuchea alienated many countries all over the world—not the least of which were the Arab and African nations so solidly behind the FUNK and GRUNK during the antiimperialist struggle of 1970–1975. The highly intelligent Vietnamese immediately capitalized on the situation and pounced on the Khmer Rouge. In the process they also mangled poor Kampuchea. Today the entire world is acquainted with the methods they used and the tragic results of their incursion.

At United Nations headquarters in January, 1979, a good number of diplomats (Arabs, Africans, even Europeans, including the Yugoslavians, particularly devoted friends of Cambodia's) assured me that if the Khmer Rouge had empowered me to handle the painful Kampuchea-Vietnam crisis at the opportune moment, "there would have been a way out." Even the Chinese leaders went so far as to tell me how bitter they were about not being able to persuade the Khmer Rouge leaders (Pol Pot and Ieng Sary) to avail themselves of my services. While I was in New York in January, 1979, to represent Democratic Kampuchea at the special session of the U.N. Security Council dealing with the Kampuchea-Vietnam dispute, some of the ambassadors present did not mince words:

—The ambassador from Guinea told me: "Thirteen out of the fifteen members of the Security Council voted for you; only the Soviets and the Czechs were against. This is a victory for you, Prince Sihanouk. Many of the U.N.'s member countries are breaking off with the Khmer Rouge for good. You are well liked and respected, Prince Sihanouk. That is why the member countries kept quiet, so as not to hinder you in the Security Council and on the international scene. If you were not here as the representative of Democratic Kampuchea, we would come out and say that that government only got what was coming to it"—meaning the punishment inflicted by Vietnam.

—The ambassador from Kuwait, along with the representative from Bangladesh, came to see me one evening in my suite at the Waldorf-Astoria. Pointing to his colleague, the Kuwait diplomat told me; "Both of us voted for you in the Security Council, Prince Sihanouk, and not for the Khmer Rouge you are here representing." His frankness was all the more remarkable for the fact he announced this in front of the Khmer Rouge ambassadors Thiounn Prasith and Keat Chhon as well as my wife Monique and myself.

—The Yugoslavian ambassador summed up the situation. He told me and my wife: "Our Khmer Rouge comrades have made a mess of things. We Yugoslavians have always done everything we could to help them out in terms of international diplomacy. We cannot sanction Vietnam's brutal invasion of Democratic Kampuchea, but the Khmer Rouge's domestic policy, victimizing their own Khmer people, cannot be justified any more than the Vietnamese army's invasion of your country can . . . Speaking of the Vietnamese, it may sound strange but here at the U.N. their diplomats told anyone who would listen that Vietnam had always held you in respect, esteem, and admiration, Your Majesty! The Vietnamese keep telling us that if Prince Sihanouk were the head of Kampuchea's government, things would never have come to this!"

I am totally devoid of personal ambition, especially now that with age, and after having undergone many of the most painful experiences possible, I see the inanity of all the effort I poured into serving my country in the past. I did, however, break the silence of my Phnom Penh confinement on one occasion. That was in January, 1978, shortly after the Vietnamese army's first large-scaled invasion of Kampuchea. I offered my services to the Khmer Rouge. They rejected my offer, saying they had just won an even greater victory than on April 17, 1975!

12 THE MYSTERY OF THE FABLED KHMER ROUGE VICTORY OF JANUARY 6, 1978

Socialist Vietnam's first blitzkrieg in Democratic Kampuchea was launched in late December, 1977, to early January, 1978. Then it fizzled out. The Vietnamese soldiers and their armored units had attacked Pol Pot's men on several fronts (Ratanakiri, Mondolkiri, Kratié, Kompong Cham, Prey Veng, Svay Rieng—including the "Parrot's Beak"— Kandal, Takeo, Kampot: almost the entire length of the Vietnam–Kampuchea border, from the high plateaus to the Gulf of Siam). On the Prey Veng–Svay Rieng front, the invaders had advanced as far as the town of Neak Luong, on the Mekong about fifty kilometers from Phnom Penh.

Still, the first North Vietnamese blitz was nothing but fireworks. When Giap's armored and infantry units reached Saigon, all they did was round up some Khmer Rouge supplies and slaves (euphemistically referred to as "members of the cooperatives" by the Pol Pot–Ieng Sary regime) and head straight back to Vietnam. The retreat of the conquering Vietnamese from Neak Luong was immediately followed by that of other troops on all fronts.

According to Radio Hanoi, which incidentally made no mention of the military penetration into Kampuchea, Vietnam was only exercising its right to self-defense, since it had been "the victim of repeated and extremely deadly Khmer Rouge incursions" into "many provinces" of South Vietnam along the Cambodian border.

Be that as it may, the major foreign radio newscasts (Voice of America, Deutsche Welle, BBC, etc.) maintained that large and bloody battles really did take place, causing tremendous human as well as material losses. Hanoi and Phnom Penh broadcasts agreed on at least one point: each army committed innumerable atrocities, including some involving innocent civilians, particularly old people, women, and children. It should be pointed out, however, that some of the details of these atrocities, broadcast day after day by the Khmer Rouge radio, strain credulity, to say the least. Pol Pot and Ieng Sary's propaganda machine would stress the Viet soldiers' rape of old Khmer women. It is obvious, however, that there were enough young Vietnamese women around to satisfy Giap's sex-starved soldiers, if need be. Would the Vietnamese, even if motivated by revenge, have been physically able to go through with the sexual violation of wizened, toothless Khmer peasant women? Still, some of these women were heard to protest over Radio Phnom Penh that they had been "savagely raped" by innumerable Vietnamese soldiers!

All this notwithstanding, it should be kept in mind that historically the warring Vietnamese have showed no mercy on the Khmers. The moral of the story is that there certainly must have been daily exchanges of atrocities and counteratrocities between the two opposing armies and the two neighbor peoples.

Another obvious fact is that as they retreated from Kampuchea after January 6, 1978, the Vietnamese were careful to take along a host of Khmer men and women who were "members of the cooperatives" set up by the Pol Pot regime. According to Radio Hanoi, they "had freed themselves" through their own efforts and fled to South Vietnam. But Radio Phnom Penh retorted that the Kampuchéan refugees in Vietnam (some 150,000) had been forcibly marched there by the invading Vietnamese troops as they beat a hasty retreat. The fact is that the Vietnamese used these 150,000 Khmer refugees to furnish the FUNSK (United National Salvation Front of Kampuchea) with more or less volunteer supporters. They were also supposed to lend credibility to the "Kampuchean popular movement" in opposition to Pol Pot and Ieng Sary—and to the People's Republic of China!

International political analysts studying the Vietnamese invasion of December, 1977, to January, 1978, seem to agree that this first Vietnamese blitzkrieg was a failure compared to the second. That was the opinion of the major foreign radio networks, particularly Voice of America. Their conclusions were based on the following facts:

—The Vietnamese high command had underestimated the strength of the Khmer Rouge's ordinary troops, and sent rather green South Vietnamese recruits to fight against Pol Pot's soldiers. The South Vietnamese were not only less seasoned but also less courageous than the North Vietnamese. Young South Vietnamese who have since fled their country have confirmed the fact their Hanoi used their contemporaries as recruits.

—When they launched their first blitzkrieg against Kampuchea, the Viets hoped it would engender a mass uprising of the Khmer people throughout the villages, so-called cooperatives, and hard labor camps. Contrary to Hanoi's strategic planning, however, no uprising took place. Thus as the Vietnamese offensive crossed provinces and occupied cities, it did not have the crucial support of the native population.

—Despite the Pol Pot regime's bad record on human rights, international opinion swiftly and decisively censured the Vietnamese invasion of Kampuchea. Faced with practically unanimous disapproval, the Vietnamese were forced to withdraw.

Although their first blitz was a defeat on the surface, the Vietnamese learned a number of valuable lessons from it, enabling them to trounce the Phnom Penh government one year later almost to the day (January 7, 1979). Their victory was so resounding that the Khmer Rouge leaders had to abandon "their" capital and form a guerrilla army. How did Hanoi turn defeat into the masterful victory of January, 1979? By way of explanation, I offer the following observations.

THE POL POT CAMP'S OVERWEENING PRIDE AFTER
JANUARY 6, 1978, LED TO SERIOUS MISJUDGMENTS OF
THE ENEMY:
January 6 became an "historic date" on the Khmer Rouge's national calendar. A government decree proclaimed the "Victory of January 6, 1978" even greater and more important than that of April 17, 1975. Incidentally, this meant the Khmer Rouge were contradicting themselves, since they had said earlier that American imperialism was the number-one military power in the world and that the Vietnamese would never have been able to defeat the Americans without the help of the Khmer Rouge. If the Vietnamese were nothing compared to the Americans, then it is hard to see why the Khmer Rouge victory over Vietnam was more glorious than their victory over the United States!

I think this was the Pol Pot regime's unwitting admission that their April 17, 1975, victory over American imperialism was far from being a 100 percent Khmer Rouge operation. Let me reiterate that the Vietnamese were behind the Khmer resistance effort from March 18, 1970, on, an important factor in the eventual victory over the U.S. and Lon Nol. The historic truth is that Kampuchea was liberated with Vietnamese help, and not that Saigon and South Vietnam were liberated with Khmer Rouge help. In fact, between 1970 and 1975 the Khmer Rouge did everything in their power to trip up their Yuon comrades!

The Khmer Rouge were blinded by pride and self-conceit. From January 6, 1978 on, their propaganda machine never stopped cranking out the slogan proclaiming Democratic Kampuchea ten times, a hundred times stronger than Socialist Vietnam, and calling the Khmer Rouge leaders the "most serious, just, clear-sighted, extraordinary" in the world.[1] This is how the Khmer Rouge army, cadres, and party members came to believe it would be impossible for the Viets to take revenge on them and win.

OSTRICHLIKE, THE POL POT GOVERNMENT REFUSED TO FACE CERTAIN UNPLEASANT REALITIES.
I will cite one of many examples: insidious and persistent Vietnamese infiltration into a certain number of border zones, especially the one known as "203." After their supposed total withdrawal from Kampuchea after January 6, 1978, the Viets were in fact able to establish and consolidate impregnable military bases in some of Kampuchea's strategic sectors—in the "Parrot's Beak," the rubber plantations of Kompong Cham and Kratié, part of the provinces of Ratanakiri (O Yadao) and Mondolkiri, etc.

As best it could without being too direct, Radio Peking called the Kampucheans' attention to Vietnam's slow, subtle, but nonetheless real infiltration of their country. Simultaneously, China wanted to alert its friends to the "silent" conquest of Kampuchean territory. Radio Peking's listeners, then, were given a very clear day-by-day picture of the

[1] In Khmer, *Moha Trem Treuv, Moha Phlu Svang, Moha Aschar.*

Vietnamese territorial gains. Yet Pol Pot's government imperturbably continued to broadcast that it was not losing ground, not even one inch . . . Radio Phnom Penh made energetic daily announcements of clearcut victories over the "chickenhearted" Vietnamese. It seems the "Yuons" were so frightened at the thought of doing battle with the Khmer Rouge that Vietnamese artillerymen had to be chained to their cannons; otherwise the Vietnamese artillery would have consisted of unmanned guns!

THE INVOLUNTARY BUT NONETHELESS REAL
CREATION OF TWO CLASSES OF KAMPUCHEAN
SOLDIERS AND FIGHTING UNITS:
Toward the end of their reign in Phnom Penh, the increasingly suspicious Pol Pot and Ieng Sary sowed discontent in a good part of their own army by making a distinction between the trusted "unconditional" units of the Nirdey or southwest military region (Kompong Speu, Takeo, Kampot) and soldiers in other regions, who were deemed less trustworthy. There was also a distinction between the six "superdivisions" protecting Pol Pot and Ieng Sary in and around the capital, and the "ordinary" divisions sent to die on the front lines. The ordinary divisions were fed less, equipped with less modern arms, and had less firepower than the superdivisions of the Praetorian Guard.

The *yotheas* from Kompong Speu province's Phnom Aural (Mt. Aural) region were the regime's favorites. It seems that during the Khmer Rouge's anti-Sihanouk struggle of the 1960s, the inhabitants of the remote and supposedly neglected villages in Kompong Speu (in southwest Cambodia, one of the country's poorer provinces), unlike the majority of peasants in the rest of Cambodia, joined in the Khmer Rouge revolution spontaneously, totally—body and soul, in a word—and were willing to do anything and everything to advance Pol Pot's cause.

During the first Vietnamese blitz, the Nirdey (Southwest) troops proved the toughest of all the Khmer Rouge units. They were consequently granted the supreme honor of surrounding Phnom Penh like a safety belt, policing the capital (which included guarding Norodom Sihanouk and Penn Nouth in their "luxury prisons"), and last but not least taking various punitive measures against the "undisciplined elements" of the revolutionary army, particularly those in Zone 203 on the South Vietnam border (which was once the home of Heng Samrin, Chea Sim, and Ros Samay of the current Phnom Penh regime).

POL POT AND IENG SARY NEVER SEEMED
AWARE OF THEIR REGIME'S MANY
ACHILLES HEELS.
Here is a sampling:

• *Pol Pot's folly was the simultaneous pursuit of two contradictory and incompatible goals.* On the one hand, Pol Pot and Ieng Sary intended to build a "Democratic" Kampuchea without delay. It would be ten times stronger than Socialist Vietnam from every point of view: military, economic, social, etc. On the other hand, they engaged Vietnam in all-directional armed confrontations, among the features of which were terrorist expeditions and counterexpeditions based on the sinister slogan "Kill everything, burn everything, destroy everything."

Adolf Hitler, Pol Pot and Ieng Sary's hero, was much more clearheaded in the 1930s than his Kampuchean disciples were in the 1970s. The first thing Hitler did after seizing power was to consolidate that power, rebuild Germany's economy, and build an army that was increasingly better trained and outfitted . . . Only after meeting these three peacetime objectives did Hitler begin to challenge neighboring countries, growing bolder year by year. In 1933 he was Chancellor of the Reich; Germany's head of State in 1934; the Austrian Anschluss took place in 1938; Czechoslovakia was taken next, first the Sudetenland, then Bohemia and Moravia in 1939; then came Danzig and the invasion of Poland.

• *The first Vietnamese blitz cost the Khmer Rouge one-third of their armed ranks,* in other words 30,000 men put permanently out of commission, according to estimates by international commentators and major radio news bureaus (particularly the Voice of America and Deutsche Welle). It would seem the Vietnamese losses were comparable. The fact remains, however, that Vietnam has a population of 50 million and 600,000 soldiers in its armed forces, not counting the approximately 1 million auxiliaries in the militia. Pol Pot and Ieng Sary's Kampuchea had only 5 million inhabitants and an army of 90,000.

• *As Pol Pot, Ieng Sary, and Khieu Samphan admitted over Radio Phnom Penh between 1976 and 1978 "the CIA, the KGB, and Vietnamese agents* made repeated attempts" to overthrow them. This means that the split within the Khmer Rouge party and army was widening. I have not been able to discover the real reasons behind this split; Khieu Samphan would not discuss it with me. All he would say was that "the Le Duan–Pham Van Dong clique" was stubbornly opposed to the Khmer Rouge leaders, and that the Vietnamese wanted to replace them with traitors to Kampuchea and the Khmer Rouge Communist revolution. The new leaders would sell Kampuchea out to

Vietnam; Vietnam would see its long-time dream of a federated Indochina come true.

To achieve their goal, Khieu Samphan explained, the Vietnamese had appealed to the Soviets and even the CIA to help them assassinate the Democratic Kampuchean regime's leaders, subsequently eliminating Kampuchea's independence and territorial integrity, exterminating the Khmer people. Radio Hanoi retorted that "the government of the Socialist Republic of Vietnam played no role at all in this purely Kampuchean matter," and that it was obviously a question of an "internal political crisis due to the people's inability to endure the Pol Pot regime's reign of terror and genocide any longer (the 'non-reactionary' elements of the Khmer Rouge party and army share these sentiments)."

Be that as it may, by 1977 Pol Pot's regime had weakened, and Radio Phnom Penh let it slip out by broadcasting the surprising news of "the complete removal of Vietnamese, CIA, and KGB agents from every cooperative, administrative department, and army unit." Also mentioned were the "inadmissible deficiencies in some of the *Kammaphibal*s"—party cadres, army officers, administration heads, etc.

Curiously enough, in 1978 a Khmer-language broadcast over Radio Peking mentioned extensive and radical purges in Zone 203; according to the same source, the "only three survivors of the purges" were none other than Heng Samrin, Chea Sim, and Ros Samay, later the three main leaders of the Vietnamese-backed People's Republic of Kampuchea.

The 1977 shake-up in Pol Pot's party brings to mind a similar one in Sihanouk's Sangkum in 1969. Lon Nol was Sihanouk's Heng Samrin, selling Cambodia out to Richard Nixon's United States. With his powerful allies' help, Lon

Nol was able to overthrow Sihanouk's regime in March, 1970. Broadcasts from Phnom Penh in 1977 kept announcing Pol Pot's regime would last not five years like Lon Nol's, but five centuries, fifty centuries, five hundred centuries. The harsh reality of the shake-up, however, belied their claims.

• *According to Pol Pot's supporters, "in two thousand years" the Kampuchean nation had never been more unified,* stronger, more powerful, than under Communist rule. The truth was something else again, in 1978. Radio Hanoi reported that by then Pol Pot and Ieng Sary had already liquidated three million Kampuchean men and women. Probably an exaggeration, but even if Pol Pot and Ieng Sary had done away with only a million and a half of their compatriots between 1975 and 1978, it would have been enough to presage the regime's stinging defeat in the face of a new Hanoi blitzkrieg. The more so since the remaining five million Khmers were barely holding on after three years of forced labor, hardships of every variety, and suffering unparalleled in all of human history! To this dismal picture we should add what the regime's "slaves" went through in order to flee Pol Pot's living hell. The "slaves" were former students, defrocked Buddhist monks, doctors or civil servants under the old regime, former soldiers of Lon Nol's, members of the bourgeoisie, ex-capitalists, who had somehow managed to survive the genocide of the "enemy classes," or else they were peasant opponents of Communism. They threaded their way through minefields and other deadly obstacles in a desperate attempt to reach the border and recover their freedom.

According to the Khmers herded into the refugee camps at Aranyaprathet (Thailand), barely one-tenth of the fugitives made it across the border . . . Kampuchea's population has been drained by the enormous number of deaths, the refugees scattered around the world. Even the military and the civilian party organization were skimmed. So were some of Pol Pot and Ieng Sary's ministers: for instance Hou Yuon (Minister of Internal Affairs and Cooperatives), Hu Nim (Minister of Information and Propaganda, and "elected" member of Democratic Kampuchea's Popular Assembly), Sar Phim (Vice President of the State Presidium and one of the main party leaders in the provinces), Koy Thuon (Minister of Finance and Commerce), Toch Phoeun (Minister of Public Works), Sien An (one of the deans of the Kampuchean Communist movement and former FUNK-GRUNK ambassador to Hanoi).

Another Khmer Rouge practice was to send prominent non-Communist members of the 1970–1975 FUNK and GRUNK governments to so-called specialized cooperatives, where they were given the most demeaning jobs (for example, the daily collection of human excrement to be made into fertilizer).

I saw only two of them again, at a banquet in my honor given in 1978: Sarin Chhak (a former member of the FUNK political bureau and the GRUNK Foreign Affairs Minister), and Gen. Duong Sam Ol (also a former member of the FUNK political bureau and GRUNK Armaments Minister). Both of them were so thin and deathly pale I hardly knew them.

• *Ieng Sary overdid his job.* The master planner of Democratic Kampuchea's foreign policy took it upon himself to purge former government officials just when his country was most in need of seasoned and popular diplomats as international representatives. Sarin Chhak, Chea San, Sisowath Methavi, Chem Snguon, Huot Sambath, Ang

Kim Khoan, had been silenced, not to mention Sihanouk and Penn Nouth. It was a case of professional jealousy and class rivalry. Still unsatisfied, Ieng Sary eliminated nearly all the Sihanouk-supporting nationalists and former members of the FUNK government who took the ill-advised step of returning to Kampuchea after the victory of April 17, 1975, even though he needed their help to get things running smoothly.

It is quite obvious that the Khmer Rouge never really wanted to set up an administration and a central government worthy of the name. In fact the country was run by four people: Pol Pot, Ieng Sary, Mme. Pol Pot, and Mme. Ieng Sary. The other members of the administration—Khieu Samphan, Son Sen, and Von Vet (Vice Premier in Charge of Economic Policy)—were little better than bit players. By the end of 1978, Von Vet too had disappeared, disposed of in one way or another.

Since they hated the Khmer monarchy, particularly Norodom Sihnouk, even more than the Vietnamese, Democratic Kampuchea's four dictators made the childish mistake of spending precious hours of each day and night writing endless and useless diatribes against the Sankgum. Meanwhile, North Vietnam's leaders, Pham Van Dong, Le Duan, and Vo Nguyen Giap, were not wasting any time denigrating and insulting their ex-Emperor Bao Dai or the late Ngo Din Diem. They concentrated all their energy on waging the war against Democratic Kampuchea, with Soviet help.

• *The elimination of competent personnel:* Non-Communist intellectuals, engineers, technicians—even Communist ones who did not show enough enthusiasm for Pol Pot and Ieng Sary's politics—were eliminated. This made it exceedingly difficult to have Kampucheans operating the industrial equipment and sophisticated weaponry sent by China. Pol Pot asked the Chinese to perform an impossible, super-Herculean task in Kampuchea: modernizing and developing the "new" Kampuchea at one fell swoop, and with practically nothing to go on. The only givens were: an exhausted population; a country with no higher- or even secondary-education system left; a nation without experienced diplomats, with no technicians or scientists; an army with no officers or junior officers having even a basic grasp of mathematics, technology, ballistics, mechanics. Everything everywhere was a complete mess.

The Chinese also found it difficult if not impossible to find and train Kampucheans to run factories, take charge of the artillery, armored divisions, and especially aviation. All during the Kampucheo-Vietnamese war, and even in 1978, not one Chinese MIG fighter plane was operational: it was all Pol Pot's pilots could do to handle the obsolete old crates Lon Nol's air force had left behind in 1975.

The American helicopters the Khmer Rouge inherited gave rise to some tragicomic incidents. Let me cite two examples:

Shortly after the April, 1975, victory, the Khmer Rouge army decided to try out a few of the American helicopters Lon Nol had abandoned in Phnom Penh. They reasoned that if they had been able to teach themselves to drive, they would be able to figure out helicopters, too. A group of young *yothea*s told Mme. Penn Nouth (wife of the former GRUNK Prime Minister) that one mechanically gifted comrade of theirs had indeed been able to get a helicopter off the ground, but he could not manage to land it. The would-be pilot finally met a far-from-heroic death when his craft ran out of fuel and crashed.

After this bizarre accident, the high command was forced to call on Capt. Pech Lim Khuon, a former pilot in Lon Nol's army who had joined the resistance movement at the beginning of the 1970–1975 war. The captain had no trouble getting airborne, and proceeded to make a happy landing in Thailand. He was subsequently granted asylum in France.

• *Without the Chinese government's wise advice and diplomatic help, Pol Pot's army would have been even easier for Gen. Giap to beat.* Democratic Kampuchea would also have been fighting Thailand.

As my readers will recall, immediately after the Khmer Rouge's 1975 victory, Son Sen (Vice Premier and Defense Chief) declared that his army wanted to win back the supposedly Khmer provinces lost to Siam (alias Thailand) over the centuries.

When the Khmer Rouge said they could walk all over the Thais, they were not exaggerating. Frequent unchecked incursions into Thai territory from late 1975 to late 1977 would demonstrate the truth of their statement. What is more, the tiny Khmer navy easily stymied the impressive navy of His Majesty the King of Thailand, and in Thailand's territorial waters at that.

On land, the Thai infantry prudently retreated from the black-clad Khmer Rouge. Thai artillery settled for shooting at the "assailants" from a healthy distance. The Thai air command announced successful strafings and bombings of the Kampuchean "revolutionary" forces. But they chose no-man's-land targets instead of directly attacking the dreaded Khmer Rouge, who had triumphed over Uncle Sam's best B-52s and F-5s. Better safe than sorry!

As a result, the Khmer Rouge virtually annexed a rather large strip of territory along the Thai-Kampuchean border, holding it until early 1978. All through this small-scale Anschluss in Thailand the fierce Khmer fighters in their black pajama outfits displayed their usual cruelty. The Bangkok government documented the atrocities, publishing a "white paper" complete with photographs to be distributed at the U.N. and around the world.

The Khmer Rouge's rather dangerous romps through Thailand seriously handicapped their anti-Vietnamese operations. Well aware that the Vietnamese are not to be toyed with, China did its best to get Pol Pot, Ieng Sary, and Son Sen to stop fooling around on the Thai frontier and concentrate their war effort more seriously on the Kampucheo-Vietnamese border. China's wise advice was eventually heeded. In 1978, as the threat to the Phnom Penh government grew more acute, there was a spectacular reconciliation between the Kampuchean oligarchy and the accommodating, ultra-cautious Bangkok government, which was only too happy to get off so easily.

• *Finally, the vicious circle of the Khmer Rouge's cruelty became their Achilles heel.* As early as the 1960s, Pol Pot, Ieng Sary, Son Sen, and Khieu Samphan had made up their minds to eliminate any obstacles in their path toward total domination of Kampuchea. Torture games became their principal training tool. Young recruits began "hardening their hearts and minds" by killing dogs, cats, and other edible animals with clubs or bayonets. Even after their April 17, 1975, victory, the Khmer Rouge kept in practice with a game consisting of throwing animals into "the fires of hell" (since they had no human victims handy).

I witnessed one instance of this at the royal palace in Phnom Penh, where I was under house arrest in 1976. The *Kammaphibal*—political commissar in charge of prisoners of the blood royal—and his men took great pleasure in catching mice, shutting them in a cage, and setting fire to it. They seemed to love watching the mice run around in circles, desperately and hopelessly looking for a way out, then die in the flames. They played this game every day ... And there was nothing my family and I could say to them about it. They had no use for the "soft" precepts of Buddhism.

Another favorite game was torturing monkeys, so much like humans in their reactions. Their tails were hacked off. They were chained by the neck and strangled as they ran behind their captors, who pulled harder and harder on the chain. The screams of these poor beasts were heartrending. The sight and sound of them were unbearable. But the young Khmer Rouge *yothea*s couldn't get enough of it.

One day a pregnant and emaciated bitch wandered through the palace gates. One of the *yothea*s grabbed a club and whacked her on the skull. She fell dead. A few hours later we were served roast dog—and puppy fetuses!

Not far from the palace a company of *yothea*s had a rather unusual crocodile farm. They fed the reptiles live monkeys. Every day the *yothea*s were entertained by the frightened cries of the unfortunate simians, and their vain efforts to climb out of the crocodile pit. Hypnotized by the huge beasts' glazed stare, they soon gave up and were quickly caught and swallowed.

Khmer Rouge atrocities in Thailand from 1975 through 1977, involving the innocent inhabitants of border villages, can be explained by the fact the *yothea*s were addicted to torture. For years their chief entertainment had been the physical suffering of men and animals.

But the Khmer Rouge's sadism eventually trapped them in a vicious circle. That is, making peace with its enemies meant Democratic Kampuchea would have to give up the addictive practice of torturing its neighbors. All it would have left would be genocide at home. However, this genocide had already gone much too far, meaning soon there would not be enough manpower to complete construction of the "new Kampuchea" (a task akin to building the pyramids). Furthermore, there would not be enough cannon fodder to contain the more and more damaging Vietnamese assaults. The only solution was to use the Vietnamese to kill two birds with one stone. So the Khmer Rouge *yothea*s were given the go-ahead to do whatever they wanted to any Vietnamese men and women they encountered; and at the same time the government acknowledged the inevitability of a fight to the death with the Vietnamese.

Now there was no way out. The government pursued this policy of "retreating forward" until February and March, 1979, when the Chinese army's steamroller crushed the overconfident Vietnamese in Vietnam's northern provinces. The Khmer Rouge's survival quite literally depended on it.

Today remnants of Pol Pot's regime survive in some parts of Kampuchea. The Khmer Rouge are much more at home as guerrilla fighters in the jungles than they are in the city. Proponents of the hair-of-the-dog-that-bit-you theory, they work at making the future of the Hanoi puppet government and the quisling Heng Samrin more uncertain than ever.

THE FACTORS CONTRIBUTING TO THE
VIETNAMESE VICTORY OVER KAMPUCHEA
ON JANUARY 7, 1979, WERE THE
FOLLOWING:

• *The Vietnamese are an extremely intelligent, te-
nacious, heroic people.* They have a remarkably homogenous and united government and ruling party. Experts in the matter consider their army one of the best
in the world. Furthermore, the Vietnamese never forget
any wrongs that have been done to them, humiliations
they have been forced to endure. Without a grasp of
these facts, there is no understanding the Socialist Republic of Vietnam.

Ieng Sary spent a good part of his youth in Vietnam.
He must have known that challenging the Vietnamese
meant playing with fire! Before singling out a mortal
enemy, it is indispensable to know everything about that
enemy, know him inside and out. The Khmer Rouge were
quite right to tell me how important it is never to overesti-
mate the enemy's strength, and that Kampuchea must get
rid of any inferiority complexes toward the Vietnamese.
But the Khmer Rouge government's downfall was their
extraordinary superiority complex when it came to the
Vietnamese and Vietnam. They also thought they were
better than the United States (of course!), better than their
closest allies—in short, better than everyone else in the
world! In terms of conceit, rodomontade, disdain for the
enemy and one's own allies, even Hitler had nothing on his
Khmer Rouge disciples.

Let us look at some of the Khmer Rouge's more nota-
ble displays of arrogance:

In 1976–1978, Khieu Samphan was fond of telling
me that Marshall Kim Il Sung's Koreans were "on the

wrong track" if they wanted to make their country truly communist. Kim Il Sung, he said, had raised the standard of living and developed the economy "too much." "Now the North Koreans have fine houses and cars, nice cities. The people are too attached to their new life," he said. "They will never want to start or even fight in a new war, their only hope of liberating South Korea and reuniting their country."

In Peking in 1975, we visited Zhou Enlai—already seriously ill—in his hospital room. I heard him advise Khieu Samphan and Ieng Thirith (Mme. Ieng Sary) not to try to achieve total communism in one giant step. The wise and perspicacious veteran of the Chinese revolution stressed the need to move "step by step" toward socialism. This would take several years of patient work. Then and only then should they advance toward a communist society. Premier Zhou Enlai reiterated that China itself had experienced disastrous setbacks in the fairly recent past by trying to make a giant leap forward and move full speed ahead into pure communism. The great Chinese statesman counseled the Khmer Rouge leaders: "Don't follow the bad example of our 'great leap forward.' Take things slowly: that is the best way to guide Kampuchea and its people to growth, prosperity, and happiness." By way of response to this splendid and moving piece of almost fatherly advice, Khieu Samphan and Ieng Thirith just smiled an incredulous and superior smile . . .

Not long after we got back to Phnom Penh, Khieu Samphan and Son Sen told me their Kampuchea was going to show the world that pure communism could indeed be achieved at one fell swoop. This was no doubt their indirect reply to Zhou Enlai. "Our country's place in history will be assured," they said. "We will be the first nation to create a completely communist society without wasting time on intermediate steps."

With this kind of warped thinking at the top, it is not hard to see why the Khmer Rouge were blind to the seriousness of the Vietnamese threat.

• *Pol Pot's supporters still had a chance as long as their "duel" with the Vietnamese was limited to terrorist and counterterrorist attacks.* For their part, the Vietnamese were well aware that the only way they could bring the arrogant Pol Pot–Ieng Sary government to heel would be to launch an all-out war effort along the most classic lines.

The truth is that the Khmer Rouge's supposed defeat of the Vietnamese in late December, 1977, and early January, 1978, was no such thing. The first Vietnamese blitz swept aside all the Khmer Rouge divisions blocking its way to Neak Luong, the perfect site for an offensive against Phnom Penh (as Lon Nol's officers had learned in early January, 1975!).

The Vietnamese would have had no trouble crossing the Mekong at Neak Luong. They had amphibious vehicles and ferryboats, and Pol Pot's ill-equipped artillery had nothing to fight them with. Khmer Rouge airpower was at best ineffectual, practically nonexistent. But the Vietnamese obviously had no intention of attacking Phonm Penh or taking any Kampuchean provincial center at that time. The only explanation for it is that they feared an international outcry.

Pol Pot and Ieng Sary's mistake during the second Vietnamese blitzkrieg (1978–1979) was to close down all Phnom Penh's foreign embassies as General Giap approached the capital. All diplomats from nations friendly to the Khmer Rouge left on January 6, 1979. The Vietnamese entered Phnom Penh the next day, but there was no one left to alert the world to their presence in the capital and the rest of the country. Russia and its satellite countries, naturally, were playing dumb . . .

The underlying Vietnamese strategy is only too obvious: because no reconciliation between the two countries was possible, the Vietnamese organized a two-part conquest of Kampuchea and the Khmer Rouge, their mortal enemies. Part one was the first blitz: undercutting the enemy's strength, doing serious damage to its economy (raiding stocks of freshly harvested rice and other grains, and rubber from the rubber plantations; destroying these plantations and all factories and industrial plants). Another important step in the first phase was eliminating Pol Pot's most fervent cadres, yet taking "salvageable" Khmer Rouge and the regime's slaves to Vietnam (much to their relief). In this way the Vietnamese were able to bring tens of thousands of Kampuchean civilians into their country in January, 1978. The Buddhist monks Pol Pot had stripped of their functions were able to don their saffron robes again once they were settled in Vietnam. They become ardent supporters of the revolt against Pol Pot and Ieng Sary.

As for the supposed nonexistence of rebellion or popular insurgency in the Kampuchean cooperatives the Vietnamese "visited" during their first blitz, later reports over Radio Phnom Penh contradicted this. Shortly after the voluntary retreat of Giap's troops on January 6, 1978, the Khmer Rouge complained of "renewed attempts to overthrow the government" by "Vietnamese agents." The broadcasts further called attention to the cruel and unusual punishment meted out to these "traitors," in the very same regions the Vietnamese had "visited" during their first invasion.

Thanks to their first blitzkrieg, then, by January, 1978,

Prince Norodom Sihanouk and Princess Monique at a pre-1970 "Feast of the Sacred Furrow" ceremony.

Princess Monique Sihanouk, Prince Norodom Sihanouk, Zhou Enlai.

(At right) *Princess Monique Sihanouk and Prince Norodom Sihanouk during their 1973 visit to the liberated zone.*

Princess Monique Sihanouk with (left to right) Mme. Hou Youn, Mme. Khieu Ponnary (President of the Union of Democratic Women), Mme. Koy Thuon (wife of an assistant minister and President of the People's Committee).

(Above) *February 1976: Prince Sihanouk bows to an Angkor statue of Buddha. Front row, left to right: President of the Revolutionary Committee (Khmer Rouge); His Excellency Penn Nouth; Prince Sihanouk; Princess Sihanouk; Mme. Penn Nouth.* PHOTO BY CAPT. ONG MEANG

(Left, above) *February 1976: on the road from Siem Reap airport to Angkor Wat. Front row, left to right (in black): Mme. Pomme Peang (Princess Sihanouk's mother); Princess Monique Sihanouk; Mme. Penn Nouth; His Excellency Penn Nouth; Prince Sihanouk; Khieu Samphan; President of the City of Siem Reap's Revolutionary Committee.* PHOTO BY CAPT. ONG MEANG

(Left, below) *February 1976: Right to left: Khieu Samphan; Prince Norodom Sihanouk; His Excellency Penn Nouth; President of the City of Siem Reap's Revolutionary Committee; the Khmer Rouge commander of the Prince's "bodyguard" as "head of state."* PHOTO BY CAPT. ONG MEANG

February 1976. Tour of a "cooperative" in Siem Reap province. Prince Norodom Sihanouk and His Excellency Penn Nouth are welcomed by members of the "cooperative." PHOTO BY CAPT. ONG MEANG

February 1976. Tour of a minuscule "hydroelectric dam" in a Khmer Rouge "cooperative" in Siem Reap province. PHOTO BY CAPT. ONG MEANG

April 2, 1976. In the royal palace, Norodom Sihanouk, Kampuchea's head of state, reads his resignation address to Kampuchea and to the world, first in Khmer, then in French. At left, Chhorn Han, political commissar of the royal palace, records the Prince's message. PHOTO BY CAPT. ONG MEANG

April 17, 1976. In front of Khemarin Palace, saluting the flag of "Democratic Kampuchea." Left to right: four Khmer Rouge (including Chhorn Hay next to the prince); Prince Norodom Sihanouk and his wife, Monique; Princess Norodom Mom (the prince's aunt); Mme. Buor Tal; a Khmer Rouge woman; Mme. Nav; three Khmer Rouge women; Mme. Khon, Mme. Sar Saoroth. PHOTO BY CAPT. ONG MEANG

Norodom Sihanouk and Penn Nouth with monks from Peking's main pagoda on Buddha's birthday, May 1979.

Heng Samrin's future government already had a large number of subjects (at least 150,000 people), along with cadres (Khmer Rouge who had voluntarily become Khmer Vietminh), teachers, doctors, technicians, even journalists (freed "slaves" of Pol Pot's), plus the indispensable army. Some soldiers were former Khmer Rouge now willing to fight for the "Indochinese Federation" championed by the followers of the late Ho Chi Minh; others were young refugees hoping to pay the Pol Pot regime back for what it had done to them.

• *Anyone well acquainted with the Vietnamese Communists knows they never do anything that is not well thought out, carefully and logically planned.* And if at first they don't succeed, they try, try again.

The Yuons clearly had no intention of taking Phnom Penh as part of their 1977–1978 plan. First they wanted to feel out the enemy, gauge its strengths and weaknesses in terms of traditional warfare. In addition, they judged it indispensable to prepare a solid "pregovernmental base" for their puppets, meaning Heng Samrin and his cohorts. The proto-government would need people to rule over, a civil service, and an army.

From this point of view, the partial Vietnamese invasion of self-styled Democratic Kampuchea had the desired effects predicted by Hanoi's military strategists and political tacticians. It is therefore unrealistic to talk about defeat in connection with their short-lived 1977–1978 Cambodian campaign.

It is more likely that Vietnam's plan was to mislead international opinion and at the same time encourage the sadly deluded Pol Pot regime to rest on its laurels. From their reputed defeat the Yuons came back to take over

Kampuchea completely in December, 1978, and January, 1979, showing that the earlier attack had gravely wounded and weakened Pol Pot's regime.

The People's Republic of China was perfectly aware of the nearly hopeless situation their Kampuchean allies had gotten into. That is why Deng Xiaoping kept insisting in 1978, both from Peking and during state visits abroad, that the Vietnamese might be able to take Phnom Penh, but they would never be able to conquer Democratic Kampuchea as a whole. With the frankness that is among his finest qualities, Deng did not try to conceal the fact that the Pol Pot regime would eventually have to launch a guerrilla counteroffensive from strongholds in Kampuchea's mountain regions.

Thus the Chinese government understood what was happening in Pol Pot's Kampuchea better than Pol Pot himself did. China foresaw everything: the inevitable defeat of the Khmer Rouge army during the dry season of 1978–1979; the Pol Pot regime's flight from Phnom Penh and other Khmer cities into Kampuchea's forests and mountains.

China also foresaw the withdrawal of its allies' diplomats and the thousands of Chinese "volunteer workers" in Kampuchea, and planned for an orderly retreat. Australia's state radio network, always well informed, announced that the Peking government had contacted Bangkok to work out the problem of planes and boats crossing Thailand on the way back to the diplomats' and volunteers' countries.

Meanwhile, Pol Pot and Ieng Sary's radio broadcasts were tirelessly repeating that everything was fine, nothing could be finer . . .

• *A character trait shared by all Vietnamese, Communist or not, is that they never forgot the wrongs their enemies have done them.* Sometimes they may wait years, even decades, for just the right opportunity to take their lethal revenge.

Pol Pot and Ieng Sary were very much afraid of reprisals against them, but they nonetheless indulged in challenging, humiliating, insulting, incessantly wounding the Socialist Republic of Vietnam, its leaders, people, nation, the Vietnamese race. It would seem there was a touch of madness in the Khmer Rouge leadership (and not a particularly light touch).

In addition to the unspeakable atrocities the Khmer Rouge inflicted upon the Vietnamese, especially women, the Kampuchean state radio network added insult to injury by incessantly broadcasting the rudest of statements about Hanoi's leaders. What is worse, they also defiled the sacred name of the "irreproachable" Uncle Ho (Ho Chi Minh). There is no quicker way to make the North Vietnamese fighting mad than attacking the father of their revolution, resistance movement, and independence.

Each people has its honor to defend. The Vietnamese nation, conscious of its stature, could not continue to ignore the Khmer Rouge's most blatant affronts to Vietnamese honor: Khmer Rouge soldiers would rape a Vietnamese woman, then ram a stake or a bayonet into her vagina. Pregnant women were cut open, their unborn babies yanked out and slapped against the dying mother's face. The *yotheas* also enjoyed cutting the breasts off well-endowed Vietnamese women. Vietnamese fishermen who fell into the hands of the Khmer Rouge were decapitated. Prisoners of war were tortured, then made to read speeches full of the crassest insults to Pham Van Dong, Le Duan, Truong Chinh, Vo Nguyen Giap, Nguyen Duy Trinh, and even the late Ho Chi Minh.

Ieng Sary did his part by heaping insults on Vietnam and its leaders. He did so at regular intervals, at the U.N., in China, the Democratic People's Republic of Korea, Japan, ASEAN member countries, Romania, Yugoslavia, at international conferences, and so on.

There was obviously no way Hanoi could forgive all this, and the only way it could put a stop to it was by toppling the Pol Pot–Ieng Sary regime.

In Phnom Penh I tried to learn the whys and wherefores of the Khmer Rouge's senselessly dangerous provocation of Vietnam. I was finally able to get Khieu Samphan to explain it in diplomatic terms. He unabashedly told me that "to unite our compatriots through the Party, to bring our workers up to their highest level of productivity, and to make the *yotheas'* ardor and valor in combat even greater, the best thing we could do was incite them to hate the Yuons more and more every day." Khieu Samphan added: "Our *bang-phaaun* [literally, older and younger brothers and sisters] are willing to make any sacrifice the minute we wave the 'Hate Vietnam' flag in front of them."

Further comment would be superfluous.

• *If a Communist regime is to succeed, it must have a homogenous group of leaders who work together smoothly.* The Socialist Republic of Vietnam is a prime and unequaled example. One cannot say as much for the leadership of Democratic Kampuchea.

Pol Pot is a visionary with an even worse case of megalomania than Hitler's. Ieng Sary is not a madman in the conventional sense of the term, but his personal ambition is inordinate, a variant of raging madness. Raging is the right word for it, since Ieng Sary had any of Kampuchea's ranking Communists who dared contradict or criticize him liquidated. His entourage consisted entirely of basely opportunist and particularly hypocritical intellectuals. In the final analysis, the government of the self-styled Democratic Kampuchean state was no more than an absolutely heterogeneous "duumvirate." As a team, Pol Pot and Ieng Sary were something like a crocodile and a hyena yoked together. They were working against a much better matched and more attractive team, which Ho Chi Minh's death had done nothing to break up or weaken. The two opposing teams were playing with very different handicaps.

• *Beyond any doubt, Pol Pot's army had the best, fiercest, and most fearless guerrilla soldiers in the world. But in terms of conventional strength it did not measure up to Gen. Giap's army.* The Khmer Rouge's artillerymen, tank commanders, and aviators could handle only unsophisticated equipment. As for Pol Pot's navy, his sailors were more like privateers. And yet the People's Republic of China made a valiant effort to modernize Kampuchea's army, all the more precious to Peking since it was losing its hold on Albania . . .

As far as the Vietnamese army goes, perhaps too much credence is given to the theory that modernization has made it less effective in guerrilla warfare. This might well prove a serious error in judgment. The Vietnamese army is not only one of the best-equipped and -trained in the world, but also fully capable of launching successful guerrilla and counterguerrilla operations.

Vietnamese guerrilla fighters know Kampuchea's terrain inside and out. Furthermore, contrary to what one might presume, the Vietnamese are not all that unpopular in my country's rural and mountain regions. Though they may have ulterior motives, the Vietnamese have been wise enough to show consideration for Kampuchea's people. Their main objective has been to combat the Khmer Rouge, so the clever Vietnamese have been careful to treat the people better than Pol Pot's soldiers ever would. Like the Khmer Rouge, they are atheists, Communist through and through; but the Vietnamese at least pretend to respect the Buddhist religion and its monks, Islam and its Imams, and so on, in Khmer territory as well as at home. This is of prime importance in Cambodia, where Pol Pot had monasteries and mosques desecrated and razed, not to mention Christian churches. If any mosques or Buddhist temples were left standing, it was so they could be converted into barns, stables, pigpens, or (with slightly less damage to them) Communist indoctrination schools.

The Kampuchean men and women living in the so-called liberated zones from 1970 to 1975 remember the Vietnamese as tolerant of their religious practices, in no hurry to "collectivize" them, and quite to the contrary encouraging free trade and even small-scale black-market activities that were lucrative for the common people, not just for the "capitalist bourgeoisie." The Khmer Rouge, on the other hand, subjected the same Kampuchean people to a "cooperative" system. Money was withdrawn from circulation, offenders severely punished.

Thus the relative moderation of the Vietnamese in the early 1970s ensured that at least 50 percent of the Khmers would later welcome them as "liberators" and old friends! The Khmer Rouge's behavior is indeed so notorious that the American press (probably relying on CIA sources) has published reports of "their continued policy of terrorism" in rural Kampuchea.

Why is this terrorism still going on when the Chinese have advised Pol Pot and his followers that unless they improve their image, they will make the Vietnamese look good by comparison? In my opinion, the explanation is simple: in the villages, communes, and provinces the Vietnamese "liberated" in December, 1978, and January, 1979, many Khmer people only too readily accepted Heng Samrin's measures of political, social, cultural, and economic liberalization. Pol Pot and the Khmer Rouge want to stamp out this liberalization and punish the native "collaborators" who welcome it . . .

• Some people may find it hard to take my next point seriously. But I know the Vietnamese well enough to feel sure it is valid: *After several decades of war, the Vietnamese find it hard to adjust to peace.* Once Saigon (now Ho Chi Minh City) fell on April 30, 1975, the Vietnamese were faced with a peace they had no idea how to deal with. As the international press concurs, the country's administration, budget, and national economy are still in a shambles and are not expected to improve in the near future. The Vietnamese are gifted warriors, but are not and never have been able to handle the receipt, distribution, and effective use of the substantial aid granted them by friendly nations, including Western countries, Japan, etc. They let machinery rust and slowly fall apart on their docks, in their airports, and elsewhere . . . On the other hand, the moment they are given war matériel, their receiving procedure is perfect, and they make the very best use of it!

In short, peacetime Vietnam is as awkward as a bull in a china shop, while it takes to war like a fish to water. The equally warlike Khmer Rouge found out how dangerous (if not fatal) it is to provoke the Vietnamese. Not only did the "Yuons" enjoy taking revenge on the Khmer Rouge, they also found the perfect way out the difficulties of peace, which had brought their country nothing but social, economic, financial crisis. Running a country at war is much easier than trying to solve the bewildering problems involved in a return to normalcy.

China may have tried to teach Vietnam a lesson in February–March, 1979, but apparently it did not take. Despite Peking's repeated warning of further reprisals, the much less powerful Vietnamese stolidly continue to colonize Kampuchea, Pol Pot's devastating guerrilla counterattacks notwithstanding.

• *The final factor contributing to the 1979 Vietnamese victory was the USSR.* The Soviets had an old score to settle with the Khmer Rouge. In September 1975, Son Sen told me what had happened between Russia and Kampuchea on April 17 of that year. Arriving in freshly "liberated" Phnom Penh, a Khmer Rouge detachment summarily moved to expel Soviet diplomats from their embassy and take down the Russian flag. The Soviets' first reaction was to refuse to come out of their lair. So Pol Pot's soldiers tried to intimidate them by riddling the embassy walls with bullets, then storming the building. The Russian diplomats were then forced to follow their captors, but not before undergoing one more humiliation: their hands were tied with rough country-style rope. The rope was untied only when the "prisoners" arrived within the French embassy compound, newly transformed (over French protest) into an exclusive concentration camp where foreigners were kept until they could be turned out of the "new" Kampuchea. Brezhnev's representatives never forgave the Khmer Rouge for this.

But that was far from the only reason behind the Russians' 1978 decision to shove Vietnam toward overt aggression against the Khmer Rouge. The fact remains that from 1975 through 1977 the entire Soviet bloc made a prodigious effort to ingratiate themselves with Kampuchea's Khmer Rouge leaders, hoping against hope that their friendliness, however spurious, would win over Pol Pot, Ieng Sary, Khieu Samphan, Son Sen, "1,000 percent" pro-Chinese though they might be.

Cuba, the spearhead of "social-imperialist" penetration in the third world, had scrupulously given official support to the Khmer Rouge's anti-American insurgence in 1970–1975. After April 18, 1975, its Phnom Penh embassy made every effort to persuade the new Kampuchean "Republic" to position itself halfway between China and Russia, as every "genuinely neutral nonaligned country should." Cuba's efforts were also in vain.

In order to save face and try to compensate for the bad image it had earned by supporting Lon Nol's regime in 1970–1975, the weary and frustrated USSR then decided to regain Kampuchea's friendship by force and with Vietnam's cooperation. This was in keeping with their hegemonic intentions in the third world. As far as Southeast Asia is concerned, the USSR and the People's Republic of China are locked in an indirect but nonetheless highly destructive struggle (nothing new to Indochina).

For China, it is fundamental and even vital not to have Kampuchea align itself with Vietnam and the USSR, since the latter two already have complete control of Laos. Once the Khmer Rouge firmly and disdainfully rejected the Soviet bloc's painfully obvious advances and aligned themselves totally with China, the Soviets were forced to "punish" Kampuchea as a matter of pride. That was the object of the Vietnamese invasion.

An added aspect was the extraordinary political and diplomatic success of Chinese President Hua Guofeng's

1978 state visit to Romania and Yugoslavia. It was an international event and an affront to the USSR. When Hua was in Bucharest and Belgrade, local leaders and the local press made digs at the Soviets in disagreeable if not downright discourteous speeches and articles. All this was humiliating to the Soviet "big brothers."

International opinion quite correctly assumed that in the wake of these diplomatic and political gibes, Moscow would certainly take revenge on the Romanian and Yugoslavian Communists. One English-language radio station made the remarkably intelligent and clear-sighted prediction that the Soviets would take direct revenge not on Bucharest or Belgrade, but on Phnom Penh—which is exactly what happened!

So the Khmer Rouge felt the heat of the Soviets' violent reaction, an inevitable consequence of the international success of Deng Xiaoping's government. Deng had signed a treaty with the Japanese that included an "antihegemonic" (meaning anti-Soviet) clause, and had established diplomatic relations with the Americans.

After all these setbacks, Brezhnev's government could not remain indifferent to Democratic Kampuchea, which was more and more openly pro-Chinese, anti-Vietnamese, and anti-Russian. On November 3, 1978, party and government heads from the USSR and Vietnam signed a "friendship and cooperation treaty" in Moscow. It was really a pact of alliance. Hanoi then began receiving fresh, intensive, and massive military aid from Moscow. Vietnam made no attempt to hide its preparations for war. In December, 1978, Socialist Vietnam's state radio went so far as to broadcast the news that "those who sow the wind reap the whirlwind" and that in Kampuchea "the days of Pol Pot and the international reactionaries [the Vietnamese term for the Chinese] are numbered"!

13

JANUARY 7, 1979:
A "SIGNIFICANT" DATE

As my readers will recall, Pol Pot's government proclaimed far and wide that January 6, 1978, the date of the Khmer Rouge "victory" over Vietnam, was the most glorious day in Kampuchea's more than two-thousand-year history.

My young Phnom Penh jailers told me: "Beating the Americans is all well and good, because the U.S. is the number-one military and economic power in the world. But giving the Vietnamese a good licking is even better, because we hate them more than the Americans." President Khieu Samphan himself gave me the following learned explanation: "We should hate the Vietnamese much more than the French colonialists or American imperialists, who could not have swallowed up our country even if they had wanted to. Of course they more or less colonized us, but they certainly did not intend to wipe out our Kampuchean race or destroy our territorial integrity—while the Vietnamese will never rest until they have completely swallowed up our country. Just look at Kampuchea Krom [South Vietnam]: what was once Kampuchean territory has now become an integral part of Vietnam and our unfortunate Khmer Krom compatriots are bound to lose their *pralung cheat* [national soul], since they have been forced to give up their Kampuchean citizenship . . . Look at Laos, too: the Laotian leadership is more Vietnamese than anything, with Kaysone Phomvihan (Prime Minister) at least half Annamite by birth and Souphanouvong (President) married to a North Vietnamese passionaria! The Laotian civil service, public works, economy, are actually headed and staffed by Vietnamese. That is why we believe it is the Kampuchean's sacred duty to hate the Vietnamese more than anything, to work harder than they do, and to accept all the sacrifices involved in humbling them for good."

A pretty speech. But did hating the Vietnamese more than the Americans mean that Kampuchea should have jumped out of the frying pan into the fire?

That is another story, as Kipling would say. Let us get back to the fabled—and fateful—date of January 6, 1978, glorified by Ieng Sary's propaganda machine. I use the word "fateful" because the regime's self-glorification, which grew more and more blatant over the months to come (between January 6, 1978, and January 7, 1979), had exactly the opposite effect of a "lightning rod" that would have warded off a Vietnamese reprisal. The victim of a mud-slinging campaign unprecedented in the history of international disputes, Hanoi embarked on a vendetta drawing to its close on January 6, 1979, one year later to the day.

On that date Giap's tanks, artillery, and divisions were already on the outskirts of Phnom Penh. Since the beginning of January, Pol Pot's cannonfire had shaken the windows in my prison home. The noise grew louder and louder over the days, then hour by hour. That meant the Vietnamese were advancing, the Khmer Rouge retreating.

Some members of my Peking entourage conjecture that the Vietnamese may have delayed their entrance into Phnom Penh by one day so that I would be able to leave Kampuchea safe and sound . . . on the last Chinese-operated airline flight out.

I have no idea whether or not that is true. It is superfluous to try to solve the "mystery" of the twenty-four-hour delay in the winning of a Vietnamese victory that had been inevitable since the end of 1978.

For all that, the Yuons were nonetheless happy to have obliterated their supposed total defeat on January 6, 1978, in the eyes of the world and for history. Better yet, the "despicable Yuons" proved that even the April 17, 1975, victory over American imperialism could not have been the exclusive work of Pol Pot's guerrilla troops, no matter how much fight they had in them. Pol Pot and Ieng Sary had also claimed they played a decisive role in liberating Saigon and the rest of Vietnam on April 30, 1975, but the Vietnamese showed who was really responsible with their overwhelming victory of January 7, 1979 . . .

Moral: render unto Caesar the things which are Caesar's, or end up looking foolish.

14

THE HUMAN-RIGHTS QUESTION: HOW THE VIETNAMESE AND SOVIETS JUSTIFIED THEIR INVASION AND COLONIZATION OF KAMPUCHEA

When the question of Kampuchea and the Vietnamese invasion was debated in the U.N. Security Council in January, 1979, the Russians, Cubans, Hungarians, Vietnamese, and other pro-Soviet delegations deliberately chose Pol Pot and Ieng Sary's human-rights record as the hobbyhorse they would use to justify their use of military force to end the reign of genocide, slavery, and forced labor in Democratic Kampuchea.

The Cubans tried to cover up the fact that the Vietnamese were in clear violation of the U.N. charter when they took it upon themselves to "punish" Pol Pot and Ieng Sary's bloodthirsty army and government (in the name of the Khmer people). The Cubans' tactic was to fling an intolerably rude and unfair insult at me: they criticized me for not having courageously committed suicide in my palace prison to protest Pol Pot's slaughter of my innocent compatriots! They claimed that only Vietnam's "compassion" had freed the Khmer people from the inhuman Khmer Rouge.

Representatives from Hanoi, Havana, and Moscow thought that the universal appeal of humanitarian concerns would help them consolidate their hold on Kampuchea, which had been Red enough, but unfortunately "super-Maoist" and avidly pro-Chinese. They erroneously believed they would be exonerated, morally speaking, if they exploited allegations by certain American leaders to the effect that human-rights violations in a given country should not be considered simply an internal matter. In 1978, for instance, the American Senator George McGovern generously invited all nations devoted to liberty and justice to send armed units to Kampuchea and help overthrow the Khmer Rouge government. And Jimmy Carter labeled the Pol Pot–Ieng Sary regime "the worst violator of human rights in the world."

The Vietnamese, Russians, Cubans, and their ilk, of course, have nothing to brag about when it comes to human rights, although even they cannot compare to Pol Pot's regime. Unfortunately for the Soviet-bloc nations, their attempt to justify the Vietnamese invasion (camouflaged as a "Kampuchean people's rebellion" against the Khmer Rouge) is totally deflated by the sad fact every adequately informed nation is well aware of: that the USSR and the entire Soviet bloc were guilty of supporting the Pol Pot–Ieng Sary regime, at least morally, from 1975 to 1977.

Let me give just a few examples:

—Until Khieu Samphan announced on December 31, 1977, that Kampuchea was breaking off diplomatic relations with the Socialist Republic of Vietnam—a unilateral break on the part of the Khmer Rouge—the Vietnamese Communists' state radio and press continually praised the Pol Pot regime and obligingly cited its "remarkable and important" advances in the creation of a new Kampuchean society.

—Prior to this break, one Vietnamese delegation after another had been sent to Kampuchea "to further the great and unshakable friendship and brotherhood" uniting Communist Vietnam and Kampuchea. When one women's delegation was in Phnom Penh, its president went so far as to condemn former Kampuchean regimes (including my own, no doubt) for their male chauvinism. Speaking for "all Vietnamese women," she claimed that before the Pol Pot regime came to power, Cambodian women never enjoyed the most elementary human rights, personal freedom, political equality with Cambodian men. Although in Sihanouk's time Vietnamese women had been given a warm welcome by their Cambodian sisters, this Communist delegation had the effrontery to proclaim that "for the first time in Kampuchea's history" Khmer women had found happiness, liberty, dignity, could serve in the government, now that Pol Pot's Communism reigned. Is it any wonder that no one was fooled by the crocodile tears the Socialist Republic of Vietnam later shed so abundantly over the broken body of the Khmer people?

—Cuba also sent official delegations to court Pol Pot and Ieng Sary. We have already seen how the Soviets, East Germans, Bulgarians, Hungarians, Czechs, Poles, etc., tried to woo the same Khmer Rouge they would later call "violators of human rights" (out of sheer spite).

Still, in defense of the Soviet block it must be admitted that many other nations also shed crocodile tears over the Khmer people's desperate situation. The proof of it is that these nations called for the total, immediate, and unconditional withdrawal of Vietnamese armed forces from Kampuchea, yet they knowingly neglected to mention that once such unconditional withdrawal had taken place, Pol Pot, Ieng Sary, and their "SS" would resume their horror show and once again transform all of Kampuchea into a vast gulag, an immense slaughterhouse worthy of Auschwitz . . .

15 WHO'S SORRY NOW FOR THE KHMER PEOPLE?

History would indeed judge the Vietnamese as true heroes if, following their
January 7, 1979, defeat of Pol Pot and
Ieng Sary's regime, they had announced
that since there was no U.N. force on the scene, their own
troops would act as a peacekeeping force, to make sure
Khmer citizens were able to exercise their civil and political
rights in all freedom. But instead of playing the role of real
liberators of Cambodia, specifically by allowing the country to organize general elections with international control,
all Vietnam did was establish its own protectorate in Kampuchea and set up a government and administration completely dependent on its support. Heng Samrin, Chea Sim,
Ros Samay, Hun Hen, and so on simply represent the Vietnamese. The Yuons even wrote every word of their pitiful
marionettes' speeches, proclamations, laws, and decrees—
not to mention Kampuchea's treaties and other alliance
agreements with Vietnam and Laos!

I know Pham Van Dong, Vo Nguyen Giap, Nguyen
Duy Trinh, and their colleagues very well. We struggled
against the United States together; our relations during
the "Second Indochinese War" from 1970 to 1975 were
very friendly. I am so familiar with the way Dong and Giap
think, their styles, the way they write in French, that it is
easy for me to recognize their presence in texts attributed
to the Khmer puppets.

But that is not the worst of it: in payment for the
trouble they took to "liberate" the Khmer people from Pol
Pot's oppression, the Vietnamese forced Heng Samrin's
government to sign several pieces of Kampuchean terri-

tory over to them, beginning with the strategically important Wai Island group, as well as the adjoining continental shelf, thought to contain sizable petroleum deposits. Not content with annexing part of Kampuchea, Hanoi extended its "proletarian and internationalist humanism" to inviting Laotian Communist troops to occupy several Kampuchean districts in the provinces of Preah Vihear, Stung Treng, Ratanakiri—all bordering on Laos.

Need I remind my readers how even the royal Laotian government of the 1960s, headed by Prince Souvanna Phouma, always stubbornly refused to acknowledge the validity of the Cambodian border delineation? Souphanouvong has maintained his predecessor's tradition of Laotian territorial claims on Kampuchea. Norodom Sihanouk was always able to preserve Cambodia from enchroachment by Laos, Vietnam, and others.

Pol Pot and Ieng Sary, who prided themselves on being the first leaders in Kampuchea's history to "rehabilitate" the Kampuchean nation, are now responsible for the loss of dignity, of national honor, and for infringements on Kampuchean territory. In their defense it must be said that without Lon Nol's 1970 coup all this would probably never have happened.

The Vietnamese ordered their Phnom Penh underlings to vituperate against Sihanouk because he had proposed a "new Geneva conference on Indochina" to study the return to normalcy and to work out the difficult situation affecting Indochina, as had been done in 1954 and 1961. Why did Hanoi and Moscow find the thought of a third international conference in Geneva so frightening? There are several possible reasons:

—In the first place, the Vietnamese and Russian

hegemonists are convinced that Pol Pot's armed resistance effort cannot go on indefinitely, and that no matter how long it continues he will not be able to win out over Giap's occupation forces. They believe that under these conditions Kampuchea's future is in their hands, providing the People's Republic of China does not declare war on Vietnam instead of limiting itself to brief shows of force in Vietnam's far north. And since, thanks to Pol Pot and Ieng Sary's misjudgment of their enemies, Kampuchea's future really *is* in their hands now, the Vietnamese and Russians would obviously have everything to lose if they went to Geneva.

—In the second place, Hanoi is afraid Norodom Sihanouk might be restored to power. Yet shortly after their January 7, 1979, victory over the Khmer Rouge, the Vietnamese seemed to favor Sihanouk's return, as they confided to certain foreign powers. They considered the Prince the only person able to preserve Cambodia's neutrality and solve the problem of conflicting foreign interests in his country. Since then, however, they have seen that time is on their side, that even though other countries are still wary of Heng Samrin, they will eventually accept his being there. But if Norodom Sihanouk returned to power, he would surely remind Vietnam and the Pathet Lao of their solemn promises to respect Cambodia's territorial borders as they existed in the 1960s; he would try every diplomatic and legal means (the International Court of Justice in The Hague) available to get back the Khmer territory those countries have illegally annexed. For Vietnam and Laos, rejecting the idea of a Third Geneva Conference, opposing Sihanouk's return to Phnom Penh, and keeping Heng Samrin's so-called government in power mean gaining not only a colony but also several choice morsels of Khmer territory.

—In the third place, it helps to remember that Vietnam and the USSR have unpleasant memories of the first Geneva Conference on Indochina. This conference gave the Communists the northern sections of Laos and Vietnam, the perfect starting point for the total conquest of the two countries. On the other hand, despite the combined efforts of Zhou Enlai (China), Molotov (USSR), and Pham Van Dong (Vietnam), Cambodia's Communists ended up with nothing. They had to let Sihanouk control the entire country. During the general legislative elections that subsequently took place under international control in 1955, the Communists won only 3 percent of the vote and not one seat in Parliament. It is quite obvious that if Heng Samrin's group had to run in a new free election in Cambodia (under international control, of course), it would not even win 1 percent of the vote! Pol Pot at least has his supporters in Cambodia, but Heng Samrin? What Khmer worthy of the name would stoop so low as to vote for the Yuons' lackeys?

—To all this I would add the Kremlin's distrust, if not to say visceral hatred, of Sihanouk, the "reactionary old fox," the "potentate," the "feudalist," as the right-wing French newspaper *L'Aurore* dubbed me. To the Soviets, anything (even Pol Pot) is better than the thought of Sihanouk back in power in Phnom Penh. The Russians have long been convinced that Sihanouk is too much a Sinophile not to be something of a Sovietophobe. That is why Moscow deliberately chose to support Lon Nol's American-backed regime, and not Sihanouk's FUNK-GRUNK, during the Second Indochinese War (1970–1975).

During a reception at the North Korean presidential residence in Pyongyang in 1972, the head of the Soviet military delegation there made a scene. Despite President Kim Il Sung's urgings, during the toasts the Russian marshal refused to drink with Norodom Sihanouk, head of

state of the supposed kingdom of Cambodia. He conspicu-
ously walked over to Ieng Sary, there to represent Cambodia's insurgents, and cordially drank to the health and
success of the Khmer Rouge leader, praising the resistance
movement. As everyone knows, Ieng Sary and his Democratic Kampuchean cohorts later returned the compliment
in their own unique way. The fact remains, however, that
if the Vietnamese were once again to lean toward restoring
Sihanouk as a compromise solution to the Kampuchean
dilemma, their Soviet allies would never give them the
green light.

Let us now consider China's position. I had it clearly explained to me twice, in January, 1979, by Vice Premier
Deng Xiaoping. What he said in essence was: "There are
no two ways to go about solving the Kampuchean problem.
The Vietnamese aggression, invasion, and occupation of
Kampuchea cannot be justified or forgiven. We must fight
and keep fighting the Vietnamese until they are beaten and
forced to evacuate your country completely and permanently. The Kampucheans are a heroic and invincible people; Democratic Kampuchea's revolutionary army reflects
those qualities. The Vietnamese do not have a chance
against them. Democratic Kampuchea's cause is a just one.
All the peoples of the world and all those who love justice
firmly support Kampuchea and its people, and always will.
The Soviet and Vietnamese hegemonists have few friends.
They will inevitably be driven out of Kampuchea if the
Kampucheans are willing to go on fighting, no matter how
long it takes. This will be a harder fight than the war
against American imperialism. It will certainly last longer
than five years. But even if it takes ten, fifteen, twenty
years of struggling, the Kampucheans will finally drive the

Vietnamese out of their country. The People's Republic of China is determined to give Democratic Kampuchea its help."

These remarks by China's top governmental leader are explicit. The position of the People's Republic of China is clear-cut: no compromises on Kampuchea with the USSR and Vietnam. An all-out fight, a fight to the finish. A radical position, but easy enough to understand: just as the USSR and Vietnam cannot tolerate the idea of a "1,000 percent pro-Chinese" Kampuchea, China rejects a Kampuchea occupied and colonized by its rivals. Communist Laos has already strayed from its relatively neutral stance between the two Communist giants, and leans toward Hanoi and Moscow.

China justified its February–March, 1979, show of force in Vietnam by blaming North Vietnam's "turbulent and insolent" incidents along the China-Vietnam border. Personally, however, I am convinced that Peking's prime objective was to encourage its Khmer Rouge allies, who face a less than simple task in driving out the Vietnamese occupiers, no matter what claims to the contrary their radio broadcasts make. Deng Xiaoping hinted to me that China might once again teach Vietnam a lesson if it continued its bad behavior "toward the Chinese people." I then asked him if the Soviets wouldn't respond with their own military show of force after two or three Chinese expeditions in North Vietnam. Confident and smiling, he answered, "They wouldn't dare!"

It remained to be seen how China would make arms shipments to Pol Pot's guerrilla fighters. Deng told me it was "no problem, Thailand is helping us." When I asked Thailand's leaders about this, they called me a liar and said I was trying to compromise Thailand's "strict neutrality" in the Vietnam-Kampuchea dispute. My guess is that the whole matter will be settled privately, without the Thai government being implicated . . .

A new Geneva Conference on Indochina will not be possible without the mutual consent of the rival countries and camps directly or indirectly involved in the Kampuchean dispute, namely the Socialist Republic of Vietnam, Heng Samrin's government, the Khmer Rouge, the USSR, and China.

Strangely enough, as I write these lines (April 6, 1979), the Khmer Rouge radio network had just reported statements the American Senator Edward Kennedy made in Washington a few days earlier, to the effect that an international conference on Kampuchea should be convened to save the Cambodian people from extinction. The fact that the Khmer Rouge mentioned this at all is extraordinary, an almost complete reversal of their initial stand toward the Vietnamese and Russians. They saw their guerrilla war as a fight to the finish. Could this mean that despite their usual bluster, the Khmer Rouge are running out of steam? Only a few hours ago a Norwegian Marxist-Leninist journalist visiting here in Peking assured me that the Vietnamese could not last in Democratic Kampuchea because they would "die of hunger" and furthermore they had to deal with "rebellions" in South Vietnam.

But earlier the Khmer Rouge ambassador in Peking had made an appeal to Lon Nol's soldiers now living in France and elsewhere, asking them to return to Kampuchea and take up arms to "drive the Vietnamese out of our country." This urgent appeal to the Khmer Rouge's former mortal enemies could itself be construed as an SOS.

The Kampuchean people are now on the brink of extinction. They have suffered terribly. The best thing the Khmer Rouge could do for them would be to agree to silence the gunfire—better late than never—and let the Khmer people speak for themselves for the first time since April 17, 1975. A government that calls itself "Democratic Kampuchea" ought to agree to truly free elections organized under international control.

I am very much afraid that if the Khmer Rouge ever accept a peaceful solution to the Kampuchean problem, it would really be nothing more than a ruse to avoid being annihilated by the Vietnamese army. If the Khmer Rouge really are at the end of their rope, the next logical step would be for their Vietnamese adversaries to assume total control of Kampuchea, despite possible shows of force by China. In that case it would be very surprising if the Russians and Vietnamese were moved by any belated humanitarian appeals for "pity on the Khmer people" that the Khmer Rouge might make.

16 AMERICA'S LAUDABLE STAND

Of all the governments not directly involved in the current Kampuchean conflict, only Jimmy Carter's has dared take a clear stand in favor of a just solution to the problems under discussion. All that many other countries have done is demand the immediate, total, and unconditional withdrawal of Vietnam's armed forces in Kampuchea. The United States, however, has made specific proposals: (1) that an international conference should be held; (2) that Pol Pot's unpopular government, and Heng Samrin's un-Kampuchean government, should be abolished; (3) that general and free elections should be organized so that the Khmer people can choose whatever political system, ideology, and government they desire for themselves and their country. Here in Peking as well as during my stay in New York (January–February, 1979), I have continuously pleaded for these measures, for what I call the "Sihanouk solution." I am happy that the American government has given my proposals due consideration.

This is a far cry from the Nixon years. As proof I need only quote the March 1, 1979, issue of *Le Monde:* "While in Bangkok, American Undersecretary of State Warren Christopher stated he was in favor of an international conference on Indochina. He said Washington hoped the U.N. would find an effective way to end China's attack on Vietnam and Vietnam's on Cambodia. One possible solution would be for Kurt Waldheim to lead a mission that might pave the way for an international conference on the Indochinese question in general and Cambodia in particular."

The Associated Press similarly reported on a statement by Assistant Secretary of State Richard Holbrooke. Datelined March 6, 1979, the story read in part: "Holbrooke said there is evidence that Pol Pot's forces, occupying mountain strongholds and other areas in the Cambodian interior, still are employing brutality and terror against the population. As to whether a pullout of Vietnamese forces from Cambodia—which the United States has demanded—would result in the Pol Pot regime regaining power, Holbrooke conceded that was a 'dilemma' that would arise from such a movement. However, he said, the U.S. position is that 'neither the Pol Pot regime nor the Vietnamese-backed regime are the legitimate representatives of the Cambodian people,' and the ultimate U.S. hope is for a new independent and neutral regime to be established."

The same source, in a cable of April 2, 1979, quotes Senator Edward Kennedy outlining a similar position: "Senator Edward Kennedy Monday called for convening an international conference on Indochina, with the goal of obtaining a ceasefire in Cambodia and establishing peace, neutrality, and independence for Cambodia and Laos . . . 'The depth of suffering of the Cambodian people is one of the great human tragedies of the twentieth century,' said Kennedy. 'They face today a brutal choice of torture and murder by rival government forces or a slow death by hunger and disease. Neither the United States nor the international community can ignore their cries for help.' "

Finally, Andrew Young, United States ambassador to the U.N. when I met him in New York (January and February, 1979), Mr. Oakley, a government official who met with me in Washington in February, 1979, and Leonard Woodcock, America's ambassador to China, when we spoke in Peking in March, 1979, all told me that the "Sihanouk solution" would ensure the best possible outcome of the Cambodian problem.

The United States, then, has taken a clear stand, one that is fair to the Khmer people. But has Washington given much thought to the practical measures necessary to help our unfortunate country?

Here is what Senator Kennedy proposes: if Vietnam agrees to withdraw all its armed forces in Cambodia, the United States should agree to establish diplomatic ties with Hanoi—and trade relations. It is obvious, however, that the Vietnamese would find massive financial, economic, and material aid—and food shipments—a much more persuasive argument in favor of the "Sihanouk solution."

Still, the USSR is not particularly likely to allow its principal Indochinese client to trade the Kampuchea they already have in hand for the prospect of a completely independent Cambodia governed by Sihanouk.

As for China, it could approve the "Sihanouk solution" in the event that the Vietnamese irreversibly eliminate the Khmer Rouge, and on the condition that the USSR and Vietnam agree on a plan for their withdrawal from Kampuchea. To tell the truth, China is in a better position than the United States to persuade the Vietnamese to be reasonable, considering that Vietnam is more sensitive to military than friendly persuasion. Since China does not fear military reprisals from Russia (as Deng Xiaoping told me), one or two more shows of force in Vietnam might convince the Yuons to let Cambodia be.

IS A CEASE-FIRE
POSSIBLE IN
KAMPUCHEA?

17

The technical application of a cease-fire agreement poses no particular problem. Before any cease-fire is possible, however, two things would have to happen: first, the Khmer Rouge would have to surrender; and second, Vietnam would have to renounce its protectorate in Kampuchea. Then the following measures might be taken:

—A 1954-type International Control Commission would be sent to Kampuchea by the new Geneva Conference on Indochina or the U.N. Other third-world countries would also send troops: Arabs, Africans, Asians, Latin Americans.

—The Control Commission's mission: bringing about a cease-fire.

—The armed contingents' mission: disarming Kampucheans still at war.

—This plan would require a complete Vietnamese pullout.

How would other third-world countries be persuaded to send troops to make peace in Cambodia? And exactly which countries would be asked to do so?

Although this may seem a delicate matter, I am sure that if a Geneva Conference or the U.N. asked me to handle it, the countries of the third world would cooperate. I am not at liberty to name the countries most likely to volunteer their help to the Khmer people. All I can say is that the terms of a cease-fire agreement would be strictly enforced in my country, because we would have enough troops to control Kampuchea's local warmongers and take over the Vietnamese "policing" of the country.

18

WHO WOULD BE AUTHORIZED TO RUN IN THE HYPOTHETICAL GENERAL ELECTIONS?

All Cambodian adults of either sex wishing to try their luck at the polls should be authorized to run. All political parties should be represented, including any that might be formed between now and the time of the elections. Pol Pot and Ieng Sary, Heng Samrin, Lon Nol, the Khmer Serei (Son Ngoc Thanh), and Sihanouk would of course be on the roster. No one should be excluded.

The general elections in question would be legislative. The people would choose representatives, deputies to the new National Assembly. The first task of the Assembly would be writing a new and truly democratic constitution. Kampuchea would be called "The State of Kampuchea," without being labeled a kingdom or republic. The State of Kampuchea would have a head of state, not a king, regent, president of the republic, or president of the presidium.

These measures should prevent a new and fatal split within the Khmer nation and at the same time satisfy both the royalists—whose number has grown in the wake of Lon Nol's pathetic attempt at a Khmer Republic and Pol Pot and Ieng Sary's Communist nightmare—and the republicans, also a large group, not to mention the nationalists, socialists, and both varieties of Communists, the pro-Chinese and the pro-Soviet.

Once the new constitution was written, the National Assembly would concentrate on electing the head of state to a four-year term (that would also be the deputies' term of office). The legislators would give their vote of confidence to the government appointed by the new head of state. They would write and pass the most urgent laws, such as financial legislation and a decree providing for the formation of a small national guard exclusively concerned with keeping the peace and maintaining order within our national boundaries.

19 THE BEST ANALYSIS OF CURRENT EVENTS IN CAMBODIA

Many journalists and diplomats here in Peking have asked me about current events in Cambodia.

In my opinion British journalist William Shawcross, author of *Sideshow: Nixon, Kissinger and the Destruction of Cambodia,* is one of the best-informed commentators on Cambodia. His March 28, 1979, article in *The Asian Wall Street Journal,* entitled "Cambodia: Defeating the Greatest Enemy," is based on interviews with Cambodian refugees in Thailand. Shawcross considers it quite understandable that these refugees are unsure about the future. Some of them think they might go back to Phnom Penh if Sihanouk returned to power. Others contend the Prince's alliance with the Khmer Rouge has discredited him. But it is clear, Shawcross says, that these Cambodians consider the Vietnamese the lesser of two evils, the greater one being the Khmer Rouge. If some Cambodians have returned to their country, it was to join Heng Samrin's forces, not the Khmer Rouge. For almost four years now the Khmer Rouge and their hatred for the Cambodian people have run rampant. They have caused several hundred thousand deaths at the very least; the heavy losses they have suffered are not enough to stop them. If anything, they are getting worse, hopelessly trapping thousands of peasants in the jungle.

Shawcross quotes a Western doctor who worked in Phnom Penh before April, 1975, watched the Khmer Rouge's triumphant entry into the capital, and since then has worked with the refugees. The doctor reports that over the past four years the Khmer Rouge have appointed younger and younger cadres, increasingly violent. Pol Pot strove to create a society with no past, no alternatives. He has not been completely successful; it is truly frightening to imagine what would happen if he did succeed.

In Bangkok, Shawcross says, some think the Vietnamese and Chinese could reach an agreement on Cambodia—and negotiate Norodom Sihanouk's return to power. But what could Sihanouk do as things now stand? He would have no basis for negotiations with the Khmer Rouge, whom Jimmy Carter has aptly called "the worst violators of human rights in the world." Shawcross therefore wonders whether it would be reasonable to ask the Vietnamese to withdraw and let the Khmer Rouge take over. He thinks it would be a risky proposition, even if the object were to create a buffer zone between Vietnam and Thailand (which in any case would do nothing to improve the Cambodian people's situation).

While many Cambodians in the Aranyaprathet refugee camp think Vietnamese imperialism may help Cambodia in the short term, they hold that no puppet, including Heng Samrin, can continue taking orders from Vietnam indefinitely. The principal threat to Cambodia is incontestably the Khmer Rouge. The conflict between Cambodia and Vietnam can wait for a solution. The conflict between the Khmer people and the Khmer Rouge cannot.

I agree with Shawcross's analysis on all but two points. First, it seems doubtful that in the long run Heng Samrin will split with Vietnam. Heng Samrin's so-called government, recognized *de jure* only by the USSR and its satellite countries, scorned by the rest of the world, is fully conscious of its own nonentity. Vietnamese colonialism is its oxygen supply; without Vietnam's help it would die. I am no astrologer, but I feel confident in predicting that come what may, Heng Samrin and his followers will cling to their Hanoi creators' coattails in order to stay in power (or reasonable semblance thereof) in Phnom Penh.

Second, while it may be true that the Cambodian people find Vietnamese imperialism more tolerable than the Khmer Rouge regime for the time being, it is also true that Khmers forced to cooperate with Heng Samrin's administration—or having freely chosen to do so—live in a permanent climate of insecurity created by the Khmer Rouge's daily (or nightly) raids, their savage reprisals.

20 IS IT POSSIBLE TO BE CONSIDERED A PATRIOT WITHOUT JOINING THE ARMED FIGHT AGAINST VIETNAMESE OCCUPATION?

In January and February, 1979, some of Lon Nol's former army officers suggested that I return to Cambodia with them, "under the banner of Samdech Euv," for a fight to the finish with the Khmer Rouge *and* the Vietnamese. It was a generous offer, most certainly informed by great patriotism.

Others, a handful of former foreign residents of Cambodia, claim I was a coward because during the 1970–1975 struggle against Lon Nol and American imperialism I was careful not to fight alongside the Khmer Rouge and Sihanouk-supporting nationalists, even though I was honorary president of the resistance movement. They claim all I did was "vacation" in China, feasting on Peking duck and French *foie gras* . . .

The simple truth is that from March, 1970, on I constantly begged my great friend Premier Zhou Enlai, as well as the Khmer Rouge leaders, to let me go to Kampuchea and get directly involved in the resistance movement— although the Khmer Rouge, not myself, would of course wield governmental power. Zhou Enlai told me he was sorry, but he could not help me return to Cambodia. Among the reasons he gave for his refusal were the risks involved in traveling along the Ho Chi Minh trail, continually bombarded by the Americans. Were I to die, Zhou said, the Kampuchean resistance movement would lose its figurehead. I then suggested that I could go on a fishing junk, which could drop me off near Koh Kong, close to the Thai border. This could be done by night at some isolated, unwatched site along the Cambodian coast. I was told that traveling by boat would be even riskier because the American and Vietnamese naval forces, even Lon Nol's navy, were constantly on the move. In the final analysis, Zhou told me, I was irreplaceable in my international role and I was much more useful to the resistance movement as its representative outside Cambodia.

The Khmer Rouge advanced the same arguments to keep me out of Cambodia. The truth is that the Sihanouk name alone helped them recruit cannon fodder more easily and win the rural and urban population away from Lon Nol. They certainly needed my political and moral support. But they wanted this support to come to them from Peking or Pyongyang. They were determined to close Cambodia off to me so that they could consolidate their own power and prevent me from holding sway over the Khmer people at some future date.

Humiliated and exasperated by such treatment, in April, 1970, I decided to leave the national resistance movement and apply for simple refugee status in France. But Sarin Chhak—shortly thereafter promoted to Foreign Affairs Minister of the GRUNK—and my wife Monique tearfully begged me to remain at the head of the resistance movement, to keep the promise I had made in my declaration of March 23, 1970: to fight to the finish against American imperialism and for the total and permanent liberation of our country. So I instead informed Zhou Enlai that I had decided I would step down after our eventual victory. That way I would not interfere with the Khmer Rouge's plans. The Chinese premier answered that his government respected my decision; still, he asked me not to make it public because the knowledge I intended to resign might "demobilize the Khmer people in their heroic combat." Zhou even told me the Cambodian people "were fighting for Sihanouk" with the goal of restoring Sihanouk as head of state after the defeat of the upstart Lon Nol! He concluded: "Samdech, if you leave the national resistance movement, the Cambodian people will stop fighting and Lon Nol and the Americans will win."

Three years later, in 1973, the United States decided to stop bombing the Ho Chi Minh trail. I seized the opportunity to ask the Khmer Rouge if I could now return to my country. The Khmer Rouge representative in Peking, Ieng Sary, suggested a meeting with the "interior leaders" in either Peking or Hanoi, as I preferred, but stressed that I could not be taken to Cambodia. I refused. I told Ieng Sary that I would lose all credibility, even in the eyes of those countries recognizing the GRUNK, if I could not so much as set foot on Khmer territory.

Ieng Sary answered with a flat no. Despairing, I appealed to Pham Van Dong, the head of the Democratic Republic of Vietnam's government, to help pressure the Khmer Rouge into letting me spend a few weeks in the liberated zone—prior to a long tour of several countries friendly to the GRUNK. The Vietnamese had to make a colossal effort to overcome the Khmer Rouge's resistance to my trip to the liberated zone. Finally Pham Van Dong prevailed. Ieng Sary himself gave me the go-ahead, telling me, however, that only my wife and I would be allowed to travel to the liberated zone; my entourage would stay behind.

The point of this anecdote is to show my readers that I have never been a coward, contrary to my enemies' claims. During my one-month stay in the liberated zone (Stung Treng, Preah Vihear, Siem Reap, Angkor) there were constant U.S. Air Force strikes. Bombing and strafing punctuated our itinerary. At night our convoy crept along with the headlights out. Brushes with death were an everyday occurence for my wife and me . . . Our lives were in even greater danger, however, during our confinement by the Khmer Rouge from January, 1976, to January, 1979. Each night when I went to bed I was unsure I would make it through the next day. And yet, as the whole world can see, I was not adversely affected by my rumored fear of dying.

Today it is my duty to work for peace and condemn the war in Kampuchea, for the simple reason that the war is an anti-Cambodian one. Pol Pot and Ieng Sary's partisans are not fighting to save Cambodia and its people, but to preserve their personal power, to keep their own compatriots enslaved, to maintain the right of life and death over all Cambodian men and women not belonging to their families or political clan.

Heng Samrin and his counterparts are also Khmer Rouge. They have never disagreed with Pol Pot and Ieng Sary on the "usefulness" and "necessity" of enslaving and killing Khmer nationals, if need be, to establish the power and the glory of the Communist Party. Heng Samrin and his followers broke off with Pol Pot and Ieng Sary only so that they could switch Democratic Kampuchea's alliance with China for the status of satellite to Vietnam and the USSR!

And if Heng Samrin and his followers, along with the Vietnamese, Russians, Cubans, and others in Kampuchea, today grant the Khmer people a few basic liberties and human rights, it is only to make Pol Pot and Ieng Sary's already deeply loathed regime look even worse by contrast.

As for the foreigners supporting or aiding either of the two warring factions, whose interests are they serving except their own? But it would probably be useless—if not wrong—to blame them for putting their national interests ahead of ours. That is, after all, their patriotic duty! And it is their right to keep on fighting . . . down to the last Cambodian, if we Khmers are so blinded by personal ambition or so careless we fall into the traps they set for us.

The common people of Cambodia have given us a magnificent example of farsightedness and genuine patriotism: they go along with neither the Khmer Rouge nor the outsiders. They prefer to flee to Thailand, exposing themselves to the greatest dangers in the process, or else hide deep in Cambodia's forests, risking death from starvation, sickness, snakebite—or being eaten by tigers and wolves. That is what I call real courage and patriotism.

In today's Kampuchea, rejecting war means fighting to save our Khmer race and nation from extinction. Doing everything in one's power to flee Kampuchea, taking refuge in a foreign country, also requires courageous and farseeing patriotism. The more of us Khmers there are outside Cambodia, the greater our chances of surviving as a nation will be, since under peaceful conditions we can continue to procreate, we will be able to give our children and grandchildren a good upbringing and education. They will become the technicians, doctors, educators, scientists Cambodia will need. If we follow the Khmer Communists' supposedly patriotic course, within a few years we will no longer exist as a people or a nation, and Kampuchea will become the permanent colony of some foreign country.

We must gird ourselves with the necessary vision and intelligence to bring an end to the living hell that is today's Kampuchea, to save our Khmer race as it hurtles toward disaster.

Cambodia can survive only if certain conditions are fulfilled.

First of all, the Vietnamese and the Khmer Rouge

should be allowed to keep killing each other off, if they so wish. The day will come when the murderous Khmer Rouge are sentenced to extinction and annihilation. As for the Vietnamese, even if they are the winners of this sordid and extremely lethal combat, they will be so much the worse for it that they will no longer be able to colonize our country. And then, once we see Vietnamese strength has been undermined, we will found a National United Front of Khmer Patriots, representative enough to win support on the international scene from all countries concerned with justice. These countries will put so much pressure on Vietnam that the weakened Hanoi government will most likely agree to negotiate with us.

The Vietnamese have every reason to be grateful to Norodom Sihanouk. Seeing how much I have sacrificed for them, including the Khmer monarchy, they will not refuse to negotiate with me. Allowing Sihanouk to reestablish Cambodia as the independent, neutral country it once was would mean greater security for everyone (including Vietnam, the USSR, and China). Once the peace with Vietnam was sealed and its armed forces were ready to pull out of Cambodia, we would ask either the Third Geneva Conference, the U.N. Security Council, or those countries willing and able to do our people an historic favor, to send armed contingents to Kampuchea—to keep the peace and to ensure the fairness of general legislative elections destined to provide our country with the government and regime it really wants.

HOW LONG CAN THE SOCIALIST REPUBLIC OF VIETNAM GO ON REFUSING TO GIVE CAMBODIA BACK ITS SOVEREIGNTY?

21

Certain of the journalists and diplomats who called on me in Peking in March and April, 1979, told me that Vietnamese occupation made them pessimistic about Kampuchea's future. In their opinion it will be virtually impossible for Cambodia to shake off the Vietnamese protectorate. Strangely enough, however, they also tell me that at home Vietnam is faced with growing and nearly insurmountable problems. For instance, there is the triple threat of an economic and financial crisis, plus food shortages; it is becoming more and more difficult to find fresh recruits for the army; several towns and provinces were flattened by the Chinese army's show of force in the north; there is unrest among certain ethnic groups; the South Vietnamese opposition has been carrying out sabotage missions; natural disasters have also occurred. Is there any reason to believe that, despite all these difficulties Vietnam will find the resources to gain a lasting hold over Cambodia?

The Peking authorities assure me that the Khmer Rouge will inevitably best the Vietnam army—within a few years. Khmer Rouge radio broadcasts reiterate this belief. However, Han Nienglong, China's Vice Minister of Foreign Affairs, confided to me in April, 1979, that "despite the facilities secretly granted by Thailand" (officially neutral in the Vietnam-Cambodia conflict) "the revolutionary army of Democratic Kampuchea is experiencing great difficulties." But the Chinese statesman found cause for optimism in two developments. First, Lon Nol's old army, under the new leadership of In Tam, the one-time Premier of the Khmer Republic, and operating in the border regions of Battambang and Oddar Meanchey, would soon join the Khmer Rouge "to fight their common enemy." Second, a large group of Khmer refugees in France also seemed ready to give its support to the Khmer Rouge! I asked Han Nienlong how many soldiers he thought In Tam had in his command. "Two to three thousand," he estimated. As for the refugees supporting the Khmer Rouge, they numbered only in the hundreds.

I also asked my Chinese friend how many armed Vietnamese might be in Kampuchea at present. "Around 150,-000," he answered. This means that before China's show of force in North Vietnam, the occupying army in Cambodia had some 110,000 to 120,000 soldiers, but afterwards the number went up to 150,000! On the other side, Voice of America reports, Pol Pot and Ieng Sary's soldiers are deserting every day by the hundreds (some days by the thousands) and heading for Thailand with their arms, baggage, families.

Analyzing this information, we can see that even an eventual famine or economic or political upheaval in Vietnam could not force the Vietnamese to evacuate Kampuchea.

For my part, I am not at all convinced that military means could force them out either. We should never forget how the Vietnamese managed to best the U.S., even though their economy was in ruins and their people were going hungry.

Cambodia's last chance is Norodom Sihanouk. I am not boasting when I say this. Only Sihanouk can negotiate with the Vietnamese. But so long as the Khmer Rouge remain the legal government of Cambodia recognized *de jure* by the U.N. and an overwhelming majority of sovereign states (including an impressive number of Western states claiming to be defenders of human rights), and so long as the Khmer Rouge have the support of the People's Republic of China, they will always be a major obstacle to a negotiated solution to the Kampuchean problem.

And the longer China delays dropping the Khmer Rouge, the stronger the Vietnamese and Soviet position in Kampuchea will become. It is easy to see that the Soviets will never allow Kampuchea to fall once again into the hands of the Khmer Rouge, China's allies. Likewise, China would never allow Heng Samrin's followers, allied with Hanoi and Moscow, to consolidate their hold over Democratic Kampuchea. If their position in Kampuchea grows stronger, the Vietnamese and Russians will never agree to a Third Geneva Conference; they would have everything to lose at one, as I have already explained. And China would never agree to go to Geneva unless the Khmer Rouge were decisively beaten by the Vietnamese army, despite help from their Lon Nol reinforcements.

What about Western powers? Like the ASEAN member countries, many of them merely express their desire to see the Vietnamese and the Russians agree to a complete and unconditional pullout from Kampuchea, even if that would mean allowing Pol Pot and Ieng Sary to move back into Phnom Penh and program a new genocide of the Khmer people.

This could happen only if China were to send a huge "volunteer corps" to push back the enemy (as it did in North Korea in 1953). But physical intervention in Kampuchea by the Chinese might well unleash the Soviets' wrath; their supposed cowardice no doubt has its limits. There is really only one way out of this vicious circle; sending Norodom Sihanouk to Hanoi as Cambodia's plenipotentiary ambassador entrusted with negotiating a settlement with the Democratic Republic of North Vietnam, a settlement honorable for all concerned.

Shortly before I sat down to write these lines (on April 17, 1979), a Lebanese journalist and his wife told me of their doubts about the eventual success of any negotiations I might undertake with the Vietnamese.

But at this point what would we have to lose if we tried the Sihanouk solution? If the results I obtained were not entirely satisfactory to Cambodia, I could always be indicted (morally speaking), copiously insulted, and sent into permanent retirement. Other possible solutions could then be tried. Negotiation does no harm to anyone when it fails. Even as I write, China and Vietnam are negotiating a settlement. Need I say more?

I do not think that Vietnam will be able to defy international opinion indefinitely. Its colonization of Kampuchea is held to be inadmissible. The obvious retort is that the racial discrimination in Rhodesia and South Africa has always gone unpunished. But the current self-protective reactions of powers concerned with the reemergence of a neutral and independent Cambodia should eventually change into a "healthy indignation," helping the survivors of this tragic period drive the Vietnamese out of Khmer territory.

Why couldn't a coalition of countries of good will do for the unfortunate Khmer people today what the Khmer king Jayavarman VII was able to accomplish against the all-powerful Chams in the twelfth century? Does the word "decolonization" still have a meaning in the late twentieth century? When Senator McGovern proposed forming an international expeditionary force in 1978 to drive Pol Pot and his followers out of Phnom Penh, governments claiming to support the cause of human rights laughed at him and upbraided him for interfering with the domestic affairs of a sovereign power, in this case so-called Democratic Kampuchea. But if the "world's worst violators of human rights" are eventually eliminated in Cambodia, what excuse will those countries then have for not intervening to help an innocent people slowly dying under foreign domination?

The Vietnamese, I hope, are too intelligent to get caught up in their colonialist undertaking in Kampuchea. A neutral Kampuchea, under international guidance, a Kampuchea with friendly relations on all sides, would be to Vietnam's advantage. I think they are well aware of that. Unless I am mistaken, once the Khmer Rouge have died out completely, the Vietnamese will begin to follow the dictates of reason and wisdom.

22 INTERNATIONAL CONTROL OVER CAMBODIA WOULD NOT COMPROMISE ITS SOVEREIGNTY AND NATIONAL DIGNITY

My readers have been able to judge how beneficial the first Geneva Conference in 1954 was to Cambodia and its people. My country would obviously have everything to gain from a new Geneva conference. The participants in that first conference—namely the People's Republic of China, the USSR, the U.S., France, Great Britain, and the three Indochinese nations—would naturally participate in the new one, along with the members of the International Control Commission—India, Canada, and Poland. In addition, Japan and the five ASEAN countries (Thailand, Singapore, Maylasia, the Philippines, Indonesia) should be invited to participate, as well as Australia and New Zealand. President Tito's Yugoslavia (since Tito is the dean of heads of state of nonaligned nations) should also be represented. Let me reiterate that the current situation in Kampuchea is too complex to be resolved by simple insistence on a Vietnamese pullout.

Vietnam's withdrawal should coincide with the arrival of adequate armed contingents sent to the Khmer people either by the U.N., the Geneva conference, or fellow third-world countries. They would have a three-part mission: (1) to implement a cease-fire; (2) to protect nonsympathizers from Khmer Rouge reprisals; (3) under the aegis of the International Control Commission, to oversee the general legislative elections.

Here I must once again emphasize a crucial point: the Cambodian people will not be automatically liberated when the last of Vietnam's occupying troops withdraw. History may judge me as it sees fit for asserting that no matter how distasteful and humiliating we Khmer find the current Vietnamese presence in our country, it is the people's only protection against being massacred by the Khmer Rouge (and inadequate protection at that). I stressed that to Romanian President Ceausescu's envoy here on April 18, 1979, when he called for the immediate, complete, and unconditional withdrawal of Vietnamese occupation troops, advocating a "general reconciliation" among Kampuchean men and women of all political tendencies, and asking that the Kampuchean people be left to themselves to determine their own future, with no outside interference. I told the Romanian diplomats that lofty theories on popular sovereignty did not apply to the current situation in my country. I emphasized the fact that leaving the Khmer people to themselves would quite simply mean leaving Pol Pot, Ieng Sary, Khieu Samphan, Son Sen, and Co. free to butcher them at will. As for bringing the Khmer Rouge and Sihanouk-supporting Nationalists together in a common United Front, that would be tantamount to putting a starving and bloodthirsty wolf in with a lamb. I also quoted the La Fontaine fable about the fight between the earthen pot and the brazen pot . . . The Khmer Rouge, still heavily armed, would eventually liquidate the last few nationalists left after the carnage of 1975 to 1979.

Those willing to see the Khmer Rouge granted custody of the Khmer people in the name of self-determination are obviously not concerned with the Khmer people's more than sorry fate. Nor are certain violently anti-Vietnamese Khmer refugee patriots any help. They would rather see their miserable compatriots subjected to more Khmer Rouge genocide than sanction the Vietnamese efforts to save them from annihilation. I would like to stress that Vietnamese "protection" of our people can never be more than a temporary solution; in the long run it would be intolerable. Personally, I never accepted either the French protectorate over my country (not a bad one, as such things go) or American neocolonialism. I even made the mistake of demanding the departure of the International Control Commission during the 1960s, thus depriving my country of one of the chief witnesses and supports of its neutrality.

Once the International Control Commission was gone, I found myself without a witness to defend me against accusations by Lon Nol and Nixon's supporters. In 1970 they deposed Sihanouk and destroyed the two-thousand-year-old Khmer monarchy, claiming that I had sold out to the Vietnamese.

Paradoxical as it may seem, my new doctrine is thus the following: Cambodia and its people will not be able to live in freedom, peace, national harmony, and real democracy unless its neutrality is internationally supervised, with an International Control Commission remaining in the country for several years, and the long-term cooperation of an international army policing the country from within. Without these indispensable precautions we would be doomed to chaos, civil war, genocide, and the ultimate disappearance of our people and our state after a tragic and protracted martyrdom unparalleled in human history.

The Khmer Rouge had exclusive control of Kampuchea from April 17, 1975, until January 6, 1979. They claim to have liberated the Kampuchean people, nation, and state from all foreign tutelage and dependence. The facts, however, do not bear them out.

The People's Republic of China, sincerely and genuinely anticolonialist and anti-imperialist, had to run everything in Democratic Kampuchea: finance, the supposedly national economy, industry, defense, civil aviation, river and sea ports, diplomacy, and so on. Nothing would have functioned properly without the massive and diverse aid and large volunteer corps generously provided by China. Pol Pot and Ieng Sary's propaganda machine, of course, never breathed a word about this aid, so vital to their regime's precarious survival. Pol Pot and Ieng Sary bragged they had brought about the total independence unprecedented in Kampuchea's two-thousand-year history: what a mockery! What is more, though it was hardly China's intention, the Pol Pot–Ieng Sary government—calling itself the most *ekareach mehas kar* ("most sovereignly independent") and also the "most prestigious and universally admired" government in the world—was always in China's tow in terms of foreign policy.

Here are a few examples:

—China decided on a rapprochement with the ASEAN countries. So the Khmer Rouge's anti-American war had barely ended when Ieng Sary began making advances to the ASEAN members, former staunch opponents of Kampuchea's resistance movement. Paricularly remarkable was the Khmer Rouge's rapprochement with Thailand, the country earlier hosting the U.S. Air Force as it massacred the Khmer population and demolished Cambodia's infrastructures.

—China renewed its ties with Japan. So Ieng Sary's diplomacy immediately centered on Tokyo. One day a beaming Khieu Samphan told me with obvious pride that Japan's foreign minister had made a point of "warmly embracing Comrade Ieng Sary" when the latter arrived in Tokyo.

—China delayed its *de jure* recognition of Angola. So Democratic Kampuchea also waited to open diplomatic relations.

—China was unhappy with Albania. So Phnom Penh and Tirana immediately broke off diplomatic relations (while taking care not to announce their *de facto* break publicly).

—Ieng Sary's state visits in Latin America were only to those countries enjoying a privileged relationship with China. Moreover, the Chinese diplomatic corps arranged all these trips.

Ieng Sary's supposed "incomparable prestige and popularity" existed only in the mouths of his diplomats, particularly Thiounn Prasith, Keat Chhon, Chan Youran, and Pech Chheang. Several representatives from Arab, African, European, even American countries told me Ieng Sary's diplomacy was despicable, his propaganda annoying, and his performance mostly detrimental. Only Chinese diplomacy, they said, made up (as best it could) for the Khmer Rouge's manifest shortcomings and deficiencies. It is thus quite clear that despite China's respect for Democratic Kampuchea's sovereignty, when it came to independence the Khmer Rouge's words spoke louder than their actions.

In circumstances like these, true independence should not be confused with surface independence. Democratic Kampuchea displayed a certain surface independence. The true independence of a Cambodia completely free of Vietnamese, Soviet, and other influence, however, would not in the least be endangered—quite to the contrary—by even the long-term supervision of an International Control Commission created by a new Geneva Conference.

IF LEGISLATIVE ELECTIONS TAKE PLACE IN CAMBODIA, WHAT KIND OF PARTY WOULD NORODOM SIHANOUK LEAD?

My party would be called the National United Front for an Independent, Neutral, Peaceful, and Open Cambodia.

• *National United Front.* The term "front" means we must fight with courage, perseverance, tenacity, and faith in our country in order to see our ideals triumph.

It would be a "national united" front because my party would try to unite the greatest possible number of Cambodian men and women around its ideals and political program. No one should join the party, however, unless he or she is able to give wholehearted support to the political program outlined in this chapter. In aiming for national unity, my party would sincerely strive to cooperate in all fairness with other political parties and the rest of our nation to accomplish tasks in the national interest and to preserve peace, order, and harmony within Kampuchea.

• *An Independent Cambodia.* At the end of the preceding chapter I explained my concept of true versus surface independence. In the economic domain, I do not believe that receiving aid from those nations willing and able to give it—with no strings attached—would constitute a threat to our sovereignty.

The Khmer Rouge have claimed that to preserve our national independence we should accept foreign aid from only two or three countries. In my opinion, the more friends and benefactors we have, the less our national independence would risk being compromised. Indeed, if we depend on only one or two countries, we inevitably put our country within the sphere of influence of those powers, while if we deal with a larger range of nations or states, we have a better chance of balancing their influence. Conflicting interests, moreover, would cancel each other out, another safeguard for our national independence. The same thing would happen in the political and diplomatic domains.

As far as the economy is concerned, experience has shown a liberal, even capitalist and free-enterprise system is infinitely preferable to a socialist or communist system. Sihanouk-style socialism foundered in the 1960s. Since this Buddhist-oriented system was based not on compulsory contributions from the rich, but rather their charity toward the poor, it was doomed; the rich would only occasionally aid the poor or their country in exchange for honors, titles, or other privileges awarded by the state or the crown. Otherwise they washed their hands of the situation. Scientifically planned socialism could never work with an easygoing, high-spirited people like the Khmers. The world has seen what happened to Kampuchea under the Khmer Rouge's brand of Marxist-Leninist, Maoist, and Pol Pot–Ieng Sary Communism. Heng Samrin's Vietnamese and Soviet-inspired Communism in the current People's Republic of Kampuchea is ending in all-out famine and the Khmer people's massive and continual exodus toward Thailand, or deep into the jungle haunts of the tigers, wolves, and snakes the people consider less dangerous than Pol Pot or Heng Samrin's Communist followers.

I rest my case. Let me only say my party will adopt the liberal system of free enterprise, free competition in all sectors (banking, commerce, industry, tourism, etc.) except for agriculture, fishing, and forestry, over which the state and Khmer citizens will have exclusive rights.

• *A Neutral Cambodia.* The Khmer Republic was too much in the thrall of the U.S. and the Saigon government. Democratic Kampuchea was more closely aligned with the People's Republic of China than was good for a Southeast Asian country jeopardized by the competition among superpowers. As for Sihanouk's kingdom of Cambodia, the moment it leaned slightly toward revolutionary Vietnam, Nixon, Lon Nol, and Sirik Matak swiftly moved to overthrow it in March, 1970.

Under these circumstances, the sine qua non condition for the survival of "tiny Cambodia" (as American news magazines like to call it) is the following: under international control, Cambodia must be made 100 percent neutral. It must adopt a Swiss-style neutrality, not settle for the more flexible course of nonalignment. The advantage of the process and eventual Swiss-style neutrality would be that neither the United States, the USSR, nor the People's Republic of China would then be able to find any excuse for military intervention in our country. A supposedly active or nonaligned neutrality, however, can turn all the colors of the rainbow, from Cuban or Khmer Rouge "infrared" to Liberian or Indonesian "ultraviolet." Nonalignment would only endanger our peace and our very existence. Our Cambodia would have everything to gain in imitating Switzerland, Sweden, or Austria, truly neutral, not merely nonaligned countries. Playing at nonalignment is a luxury our small nation cannot afford.

• *A Peaceful Cambodia.* Living in peace means hating and despising war. Our future Cambodia must be not only peaceful, but pacifist. Peace must be secured (1) by the total disarmament of all armed Khmers, no matter what political camp they belong to; the international army mentioned above would handle the disarmament, regulated by the International Control Commission; (2) by abolishing all Khmer or Kampuchean armed forces, and replacing them —not temporarily, but permanently—with a small national guard to keep peace at home; (3) by international military supervision.

• *An Open Cambodia.* Invoking security reasons, the Khmer Rouge regime closed the doors of their new Kampuchea to all countries not to their liking. The international press, too, was almost entirely banned from entering. The only exceptions were a few privileged visitors and Chinese, North Korean, and other comrades-at-arms. In the economic domain the country was just as closed to foreign aid.

It is true that my own regime was not particularly cooperative during the 1960s. Very few international journalists and correspondents were allowed into our country. As for foreign aid, I tended to favor the Chinese, Soviets, French, North Koreans, Yugoslavians, Czechs, East Germans, and the North Vietnamese and Vietcong. My policy of selective and restricted foreign aid was one of my fundamental errors.

The fact that only "friendly" journalists were allowed into my country harmed Cambodia's good name. I naïvely thought it was a good idea to blacklist newspapers, magazines, and journalists unfavorable to Sihanouk and his regime. However, instead of trying to get back in my good graces, the victims of my policy did even more damage to my reputation. The undeniable and indestructible power of the international press is such that it is infinitely better to let the press investigate and write anything it wants to about you and your country if you want your regime to be respectable and respected. Taking on the international press is pure suicide.

Thus my party will support complete freedom of the press within our country, especially as concerns the opposition press. We will ask our future government not to impose any limits on international correspondents entering or staying in our country, not to discriminate in any way against national or international publications, which will circulate freely throughout Cambodia. Even the most radical Communist publications, as well as the most reactionary newspapers, will of course receive the same treatment as more moderate publications. A genuinely democratic regime has nothing to fear from subversive organizations, providing they are peaceful and not military ones like the Khmer Rouge or Khmer Vietminh.

As for diplomacy, my party will advocate opening relations with all foreign powers and states on every continent, of every political and ideological tendency. It will strive to maintain the best possible relations with neighboring countries, for peace (or lack of it) in Cambodia will depend on these relations. No matter how we feel about our neighbors, we must live next to them until the end of time!

In other domains (social and cultural, etc.), my party will support active cooperation with UNESCO, France's École Française d'Extrême Orient (for the preservation of Angkor Wat, the restoration of our museums, monasteries, etc.), with UNICEF, the International Red Cross, the Food and Agriculture Organization (FAO), the office of the High Commissioner of Refugees, with human-rights organizations, and so on. In the religious domain my party will request that Hinayana Buddhism be reinstated as Cam-

bodia's official religion, but Islam, Catholicism, Protestant-
ism, and Mayahana Buddhism will also be reinstated and
other commonly recognized religions officially recognized.

Finally, my party will work steadily and energetically
to make certain the Cambodian government respects
human rights. Both the spirit and the letter of the United
Nations Charter and the Universal Declaration of Human
Rights must be followed.

That is in essence the political platform I would propose to the voters in a liberated and independent Cambodia
of the future.

The following details complement my program:

—My party would favor a multiparty parliamentary
regime, based to some extent on France's Third or Fourth
Republic.

—The parliament would elect a head of state to a four-
year term. Legislators would also serve four-year terms.
My party would favor a bicameral system.

—The head of state would appoint a prime minister,
but would not run the government. For the sake of Cambodia's international reputation, however, the head of state
might (with cabinet approval) personally direct delegations
to international conferences. He would also address the
U.N. General Assembly each year.

—The prime minister and his or her government must
be approved by a vote of the legislature (lower house or
both houses). Unless approval is voted by legislative majority, the premier and the entire government must resign.

—All men and women eighteen years of age or older
will have the right to vote.

—All Cambodian citizens over twenty-one may run for
the National Assembly; those over forty, for the Senate.

As far as the leadership of my hypothetical or future party is concerned, it will be run by an eight-member political bureau or executive committee headed by the party chief (Norodom Sihanouk). The executive committee will be elected by the party's one-hundred-member central committee. A general meeting of party members will assign the central and executive committees their tasks. There will be an annual party convention at which each of the executive committee's decisions will be subject to approval by majority vote. The party president will decide any ties. The members of the executive committee will elect a party vice president to take over for the president in the event of his absence or illness. Should the party president resign or die, the central committee will proceed to elect a new president. Another alternative would be for the party to vote to disband.

In closing, I would like to make it clear that I have not formulated the above platform for my own personal satisfaction as a political leader. I am completely sincere in my desire to see Cambodia provided with a liberal political regime.

Between March 18, 1970, and January 7, 1979, I had all the time in the world to appraise my past mistakes. I am almost sixty years old. I have had humiliation upon humiliation heaped upon me by Lon Nol and his followers, then the Khmer Rouge. I have plumbed the depths of the indescribable horror that has been the lot of the lovable and innocent Khmer people for so many years, far too many. Through it all my people have continued to love me, and my one desire is to provide them with the means to thrive and rebuild their country, to enjoy life once more after surviving the most infamous living hell the world has ever known.

IT IS IMPOSSIBLE
TO PREDICT THE FUTURE

There are few easier ways of making a fool of oneself than prophesying and prognosticating, because the future is unpredictable. I will therefore make no predictions about the outcome of the Kampuchea-Vietnam conflict, only mention a few pertinent facts. The first is that Chinese government circles are very pessimistic about the Khmer Rouge, held to be in a "very difficult" situation. Chinese pessimism seems justified, given the rout of Khmer Rouge forces as seen along the Cambodia-Thailand border; thousands of soldiers are crossing it in an incredible state of distress. The Khmer Rouge's radio, of course, continues with its usual braggadocio. But since January, 1979, their radio network has been headquartered in Peking. Now the only danger Ieng Sary's propagandists run is overindulging in lacquered duck!

Today the question is whether China, on the one hand, is preparing to launch a second offensive in North Vietnam in an attempt to reinforce Pol Pot's faltering revolutionary army, and on the other hand if Kriangsak Chamanond's Thailand has room in its hospitals for the tens of thousands of disabled Khmer Rouge soldiers who would need to recuperate before fighting the Vietnamese and Heng Samrin's followers again.

If the Chinese army makes a second, perhaps a third show of force in Vietnam, Hanoi may consider opening negotiations with Sihanouk—it has refused to do so up till now—which could lead to a new Geneva conference on Cambodia. But this possibility is entirely in the realm of hypothesis; if I know the Vietnamese, they are not especially inclined to humble themselves before their attackers.

The only way to move them is to open a dialogue, speak the language of brotherhood and diplomatic courtesy.

Even so, it is obvious that in the months and no doubt years to come the Vietnamese will have more and more acute and insoluble problems in feeding their people. Their long-coveted Indochinese Federation is made up of a famished Vietnam, a poor, weak, and extremely fragile Laos, and a miserable, desperate, vanishing Kampuchea.

Under the Viet protectorate, the Khmer people, including those in Phnom Penh, have become the victims of a total and irremediable famine. Hanoi's propaganda promised the return of the *riel* (the national currency) and Kampuchea's markets. But after several months of being governed by the Vietnamese and the Indochinese federation, the Khmer people have nothing but edible roots to sustain them.

The question is therefore how long Vietnam will be able to guide the "radiant destiny" of its pathetic Indochinese Federation (keeping in mind that the Russians are not about to feed Vietnam, since they have to buy their own food from the United States).

Finally, the United States and other advanced Western countries are unaware of two very powerful weapons they could use to persuade Vietnam to pull out of Cambodia. One would be the promise of massive food shipments and foreign aid if the Vietnamese army withdraws from Kampuchea; the other would be to cut off all aid, even humanitarian relief efforts, and all economic cooperation with Vietnam as long as it refuses to give the Khmer people back their national independence and their freedom. Some developed countries, such as Japan, have already used this weapon against Vietnam, but many others hesitate.

I must nevertheless make it clear that I am sorry the reason Japan's current government is anti-Vietnamese is not so much that it takes pity on the Khmer people, but that it wants to help Pol Pot back into power. I base this statement on the fact that on February 13, 1979, a high official in Japan's state department I met at Narita Airport (Japan) strongly encouraged me to "cooperate" with the government of Democratic Kampuchea, help with its fight against the Vietnamese! Cutting off supplies to the Vietnamese is all well and good . . . providing it is not intended to implement the return of the incorrigible assassins of the Khmer people, nation, and race.

25 IN CONCLUSION...

In place of a conclusion, I would like to make a wish: may Cambodia, my country, live forever in peace with its closest neighbors—even if the Khmer are by nature adamantly anti-Vietnamese.

The Khmer Rouge provide an edifying example: they became close allies with China and North Korea, the best of friends with Romania, Yugoslavia, Thailand, Japan, Egypt, Malaysia, and so on. But they did everything possible to alienate and provoke Vietnam and even Laos.

They quickly got a reaction: today Vietnam has colonized at least 90 percent of their so-called Democratic Kampuchea and Laos controls slightly more than 5 percent of their former territory, while their other allies and supporters not sharing a border with Cambodia can do nothing to save their dear friends the Khmer Rouge (this includes Thailand, which does of course border on Cambodia). Some of their friends have only one course open to them: appealing to Norodom Sihanouk to "cooperate" with the Pol Pot–Ieng Sary regime within the framework of a National United Front, the broadest and most democratic one possible.

Besides the Khmer Rouge, there are also thoroughgoing anti-Vietnamese Khmers among the intellectuals and dignitaries now living in foreign countries. They are certain to accuse me of being a pro-Vietnamese traitor, just as Lon Nol and his followers did in 1970–1974.

But no matter what they say about me, until the day I die I will keep on believing that the Vietnamese will have no regard for our national independence and territorial integrity until they have reason to be grateful to us. We could begin by dropping the insulting term of *Yuon* in reference to them.

The Lebanese journalist couple I mentioned earlier pointed out to me that the People's Republic of China had also given Vietnam a great deal of various kinds of aid during the fight against the Americans, but that the Vietnamese have repaid their Chinese benefactors with nothing but ingratitude.

This argument might apply to Cambodia if the Sino-Vietnamese falling-out were not mainly due to religious differences, so to speak. There is indeed a schism within the great Communist religion. The Sino-Soviet split has inevitably damaged Sino-Vietnamese relations. When two Communist countries no longer agree on how to interpret the Marxist-Leninist doctrine, the worst kind of blood feud in the world results. Even little Albania now very probably hates China and the USSR more than it does the United States ... As for China, it would rather have relations with Pinochet's Chile than reconcile with the Soviets ...

To come back to the Vietnamese, who are certainly no angels, it is nonetheless true that a Sihanouk regime in Cambodia would be infinitely more acceptable to them than an anti-Soviet, anti-Vietnamese Communist government "too fully" aligned with the People's Republic of China. China too would rather see a regime led by In Tam, Lon Nol, or Son Sann (Han Nienlong had nice things to say about former Prime Minister Son Sann in April, 1979), than have to suffer the presence of Heng Samrin and his followers, the vassals of Hanoi and Moscow.

Friendship is possible between a decidedly Communist and an anti-Communist regime, while friendly relations between a Communist country in the Chinese fold and one of the Soviet persuasion are not workable.

There is a lesson in the events of the past few years:

we must learn from history. France, for instance, chose under De Gaulle and now under Giscard's leadership to exorcise the traditional French hatred for the Germans and make good relations with its closest neighbors a top priority. France is wise to safeguard its security and its future, realizing that it is much more difficult but also more vital to establish truly friendly relations with neighboring countries than with distant ones.

The normalization of our Kampuchea's relations with Laos and especially with the intimidating Vietnamese is much more urgent, much more vital than the far easier process of establishing good relations with the far-off countries of Latin America . . . or the less distant North or South Pole.

POSTSCRIPT

Many months have now passed since this book's initial publication in French, months of great moral and physical suffering for the Khmer people.

As this English-language edition goes to press, I find I have nothing to add to or delete from my original proposals for a just and reasonable solution to the Cambodian question.

The situation in Cambodia has changed very little since the beginning of 1979, except that Vietnam has extended and tightened its military and political control over the greater part of Khmer territory. Barring opposition from the free world, we shall soon see a *de facto* and eventually a *de jure* annexation of Cambodia by the Vietnamese.

In late 1979, I offered to meet with Premier Pham Van Dong, without preliminaries and in the city of his choice (including Hanoi), to discuss possible peaceful solutions to the Khmer-Vietnam dispute and the resumption of friendly relations between our neighboring countries. My three amicable requests for a meeting were rejected; despite this rebuff, I might add, my offer still holds.

Soviet-backed Vietnamese expansionism in Southeast Asia, if left unchecked, may well trigger a Third World War. All countries opposed to such hegemony must realize that continued recognition of the Khmer Rouge can only be counterproductive: the Cambodian people have disowned their government, and the Khmer Rouge army, or what is left of it, affords only the flimsiest of protective shields for Thailand along the Khmer-Thai border.

To end the deadlock in Cambodia, it is imperative that

all countries not in agreement with Vietnam (meaning the vast majority of countries) summon the courage and wisdom to declare (first of all at the United Nations) that Cambodia has no government, that the Cambodian people must recover their sovereignty and ability to choose a national government worthy of the name by means of free elections held in the context of a neutrality guaranteed by international control.

I urge that all governments, political parties and associations, all private citizens who feel friendship or compassion for the Khmer people, work toward this goal. I am firmly convinced there is no other solution that can save the survivors of Khmer Rouge genocide from slavery, perhaps death, and in the process no doubt spare the civilized world the expense of a new international conflict.

APPENDICES

DEFINITION OF TERMS

"Cambodia" and "Kampuchea"

"Cambodia" is the English equivalent of "Kampuchea," the Khmer pronunciation. Both terms designate the same country, the land of the Cambodians or Khmers.

The supernationalist Khmer Rouge wanted "Kampuchea" to be the internationally accepted term. That is why I have used Kampuchea as much as possible when referring to the Khmer Rouge.

"Cambodian" and "Khmer"

The word "Khmer" designates the racial or ethnic majority group in Cambodia (or Kampuchea).

In China the Hans are the ethnic majority, but there are also other groups such as the Mongols, Uighurs, Miao, etc. Cambodia also has ethnic minorities, including the Chams, Samres, Kuoys, etc.

The Khmer Rouge practically banned the word "Khmer" from their vocabulary, probably for two reasons. One is their hatred or resentment of Lon Nol's late "Khmer Republic"; the Khmer Rouge not altogether incorrectly hold that the word "Khmer" was discredited by the extremely corrupt and treacherous character of the regime of Lon Nol, Sirik Matak, Long Boret, and Lon Non. The same thing is true of the word "republic." That is no doubt why the Khmer Rouge called their regime "Democratic Kampuchea."

The second reason why the Khmer Rouge used the term Kampuchea instead of Khmer is that they did not want to make Kampuchea's ethnic minorities seem like second-class citizens.

The most fanatic Khmer Rouge soldiers were from the mountain and forest regions. Using the term "Khmer" to mean any Cambodian would be an insult to minority groups, especially since most ethnic Khmers decided to stay in the corrupt and pleasure-loving cities run by Lon Nol, the American imperialists, and other neocolonialists and capitalists from the so-called free world.

Personally, I nevertheless tend to use the term "Khmer" because over the past two centuries this term has come to represent all things Cambodian to the world, particularly the Khmer civilization, one of the oldest and most impressive in human history.

KHMER ROUGE LEADERS

Pol Pot (alias of *Saloth Sâr*): Prime Minister (head of government) and general secretary of the Kampuchean Communist Party (head of the only party in self-proclaimed Democratic Kampuchea).

Ieng Sary: the number-two man in the Pol Pot regime. Official functions: Vice Prime Minister, head of Foreign Affairs. Official functions: uncontested head of the Propaganda Ministry (after Hu Nim's 1977 "disappearance"), of Public Works and Telecommunications (after Toch Phoeun's 1977 "disappearance"); Minister of the Interior and Cooperatives (after Hou Yuon "disappeared" in April or May of 1975), of Tourism and Fine Arts (national museums, historical monuments), of Civil Aviation, Commerce and Finance (after Koy Thuon's 1976 execution), etc.

Son Sen: Vice Prime Minister in charge of National Defense.

Khieu Samphan: President of the State Presidium (head of state): honorary functions.

THE REGIME'S EGERIAS

Mme. Pol Pot, née *Khieu Ponnary:* member of an upper-class family once connected to that of my paternal grandparents (Prince and Princess Norodom Sutharot). Highly intelligent and very intellectual. President of the Association of Democratic Kampuchean Women—in other words, chief of the entire female population of Cambodia.

Mme. Ieng Sary, née *Khieu Thirith:* younger sister of Khieu Ponnary (Mme. Pol Pot). Highly intelligent and very intellectual. Speaks fluent French and English. Minister of Social Action: she in fact controlled all aspects of cultural, social, and economic life for all the subjects of the Pol Pot–Ieng Sary–Ponnary–Thirith oligarchy.

INDEX